Research & Development: Key Issues for Management

Edited by James K. Brown
and Lita M. Elvers

A Conference Report from The Conference Board

lg 8/7/84

Contents

Charts

Acknowledgment

We wish to thank Dr. Lillian W. Kay, Manager of Editorial Services for The Conference Board, and Joyce Fine Schultz, Senior Editorial Associate, for their help in readying this volume for publication.

James K. Brown
Lita M. Elvers

Who's Who in This Report

W.O. BAKER

Retired Chairman of the Board of Bell Telephone Laboratories, Inc., and Chairman of Rockefeller University and the Andrew W. Mellon Foundation. Dr. Baker's many current affiliations include the Gas Research Institute Advisory Council and the Advisory Board of New Jersey Science/Technology Center, as well as several professional societies. Dr. Baker has been member, chairman or consultant to a range of industrial and government advisory panels, editorial advisory boards, and presidential commissions. Joining Bell's Technical Staff in 1939, he became Vice President and Director of Research in 1955, and Chairman in 1973. He is a Fellow of the American Institute of Chemists, American Physical Society, and the Franklin Institute.

LEWIS M. BRANSCOMB

Vice President and Chief Scientist, International Business Machines Corporation. Dr. Branscomb was appointed to the National Science Board by President Carter and has been its Chairman since 1980. Member of a number of presidential commissions, he is on the President's National Productivity Advisory Committee and Chairman of its Subcommittee on Research, Development and Technological Innovation. From 1969-1972, he was Director of the National Bureau of Standards. He has received several awards, including the Gold Medal for Exceptional Service from the U.S. Department of Commerce. A research physicist, Dr. Branscomb is a member of several professional societies and past-President of the American Physical Society.

JOHN A. BRIDGES

Vice President, Research and Development, Aladdin Industries, Inc. Mr. Bridges joined the company as a machine designer. Named Vice President, R&D, Institutional Division, in 1976, he assumed his current position in 1982. Mr. Bridges has invented and developed numerous new products for the company and holds over 75 U.S. and foreign patents. His inventions have been responsible for the start of businesses that now account for over one-quarter of Aladdin's sales and one-third of its profits. Over the years, he has experimented with a number of organizational structures and environments which might best foster innovation. He is a member of the Industrial Research Institute.

ROBERT A. CHARPIE

President, Cabot Corporation. Dr. Charpie came to Cabot from Bell & Howell, where he was President. A former Assistant Director of the Oak Ridge National Laboratory and then Director of its Reactor Division, he was Director of Technology of the Development Department at Union Carbide, and was named President of the Electronics Division in 1966. Dr. Charpie was Deputy U.S. Delegate to the United Nations Advisory Committee on Atomic Energy. He has served on several advisory boards, is a Fellow of the American Physical Society, American Nuclear Society, and New York Academy of Sciences, and a member of the National Academy of Engineering. Dr. Charpie serves on the Visiting Committee for the Department of Nuclear Engineering at MIT and is a

Trustee of the Carnegie Institute of Technology (now Carnegie-Mellon University).

A.B. COHEN

Director of Research, Electronics, in the Photo Products Department, E.I. du Pont de Nemours and Company. Dr. Cohen received the Commercial Development Association Honor Award for 1981. Involved in research and new venture management at Du Pont since 1955, he supervised development of technology for the first synthetic photographic film base and a number of novel photographic products, which resulted in the development of many unconventional commercial applications for the printing and electronic industries. Dr. Cohen has more than 250 U.S. and foreign patents. He and his associates have been five time recipients of IR-100 awards.

MARTIN COOPER

Vice President and Director of Research and Development, Motorola Inc., Mr. Cooper was instrumental in the development of mobile telephones and radios and the establishment of extensive quartz crystal capability. He led recent development of cellular radiotelephone systems and several new trunked mobile radio dispatch systems, and has been deeply involved in efforts to allocate a new radio frequency spectrum for the Land Mobile Radio Services. Mr. Cooper has been granted six patents in communications technology. He is a Fellow and past-President of the Institute of Electrical and Electronics Engineers and a Fellow of the Radio Club of America.

RICHARD N. FOSTER

Director, McKinsey & Company, Inc. Dr. Foster leads the firm's activities in chemicals. His assignments have included the development of technology strategies and organization for major international petroleum and chemicals companies. Dr. Foster was formerly with Union Carbide as International Product/Market Manager for fine chemicals. He has served on committees for the National Academy of Engineering and the National Academy of Science. He holds two patents in the field of plasma chemistry. Dr. Foster is the recipient of an IR-100 award in product development.

ROBERT A. FULLER

Corporate Vice President—Science and Technology, Johnson & Johnson. Dr. Fuller held management positions in various R&D divisions prior to being named to his present post in 1981. A founding member of the Canadian Research Management Association, he is a member of the Industrial Research Institute, among several U.S. and Canadian professional societies. Dr. Fuller has been a Trustee of the Society of Sigma Xi, Chairman of the National Conference on the Advancement of Research, recent President of the New Jersey Science/Technology Center, and a Director and Chairman of the Research & Development Council of New Jersey. Recently, he was a member of the National Academy of Sciences Panel on Advanced Technology Competition and the Industrialized Allies, and the Academy Industry Program Advisory Committee.

HERBERT I. FUSFELD

Director, Center for Science and Technology Policy, Graduate School of Business Administration, New York University. Dr. Fusfeld was Director of Reseach at Kennecott Copper Corporation for 15 years. For several years a member of the U.S./U.S.S.R. Joint Commission for Scientific & Technological Cooperation, he has served on national advisory panels and as Chairman of the Advisory Panel for the Institute of Materials Research of the National Bureau of Standards. A past-President of the Industrial Research Institute, Dr. Fusfeld was on the National Science Foundation Advisory Council and the Advisory Committee on Technology and Economic Growth of the Organization for Economic Cooperation and Development. Formerly on the Governing Board of the American Institute of Physics, he is a Fellow of the American Association for the Advancement of Science.

JOSEPH G. GAVIN, JR.

President and Chief Operating Officer, Grumman Corporation. Mr. Gavin was given direction of the Lunar Module program in 1962, later becoming Director of Space Programs, until named President and Chairman, Grumman Aerospace Corporation. President of the parent company since 1976, he is a director and chairman of several subsidiaries. Among the honors for his contribution to aerospace technology, he received the Distinguished Public Service Medal from the National Aeronautics and Space Administration. A Fellow of the American Astronautical Society and the American Institute of Aeronautics and Astronautics, Mr. Gavin is a past-President of the AIAA and a member of the Board of Governors of the Aerospace Industries Association of America, Inc. He is a member of government advisory committees, a Trustee of the Polytechnic Institute of New York, and a member of the MIT Corporation Visiting Committee.

J.E. GOLDMAN

Retired Senior Vice President and Chief Scientist, Xerox Corporation. Dr. Goldman came to Xerox from the Ford Motor Company, where he was Director of the Scientific Laboratory. Former head of the Laboratory for Magnetics Research at the Carnegie Institute of Technology (now Carnegie-Mellon University), he also held the Edwin Webster Visiting Professorship at MIT. Dr. Goldman has served on various industrial boards, government advisory committees, and university visiting committees. Among other posts, he has been Chairman of the Statutory Visiting Committee of the National Bureau of Standards, a member of the Commerce Technical Advisory Board, and Chairman of the U.S.-Israel Binational Advisory Council on Research and Development.

MARY L. GOOD

Vice President and Director of Research, UOP Inc. Dr. Good is Gold Medalist for 1983 of the American Institute of Chemists, and was named 1982 Scientist of the Year by *Industrial Research and Development* magazine. She is Vice-Chairman of the National Science Board, President of the Inorganic Division of the International Union of Pure and Applied Chemistry, a member of the Federal Science and Technology Committee of the Industrial Research Institute, among several other affiliations. Past Chairman of the Board of Directors of the American Chemical Society, Dr. Good has served on several national advisory panels. She was Boyd Professor of Chemistry at the University of New Orleans, then Boyd Professor of Materials Science, Louisiana State University.

LEON C. GREENE

Vice President, New Compound Evaluation and Licensing, Worldwide Pharmaceuticals, Smith Kline & French Laboratories. Dr. Greene was named Vice President of Worldwide Development in 1971, then Vice President, Development—U.S., Canada, Latin America, Far East, and more recently, Vice President, New Product Technology. Prior to joining the organization, he was a physiologist for the U.S. government. He was Professor of Biological Sciences at Drexel University, and has been an Associate in Physiology at the University of Pennsylvania since 1958. Member of a number of professional societies, Dr. Greene is a Fellow of the Philadelphia College of Physicians.

GEORGE A. KEYWORTH, II

Science Advisor to the President and Director, Office of Science and Technology Policy. Dr. Keyworth came to the White House from Los Alamos Scientific Laboratory, where he focused on fundamental research in nuclear physics. He developed an experimental program which led to a major breakthrough in the understanding of resonance fission, in addition to providing a new technique for nuclear spectroscopy. Dr. Keyworth led a comprehensive program in nuclear and fundamental interaction physics. In 1978, he became head of the experimental physics division and later assumed direction of the diagnostic program of underground nuclear tests at the Nevada Test Site. He is a Fellow of the American Physical Society and the American Association for the Advancement of Science.

ROBERT H. KRIEBLE

Chairman and Chief Executive Officer, Loctite Corporation. Mr. Krieble was previously a research chemist at General Electric, then General Manager of GE's Chemical Development Department. He joined Loctite as Vice President in 1956. The inventor of several patents in the fields of silicones, anaerobic adhesives and petrochemicals via air oxidation, Mr. Krieble has received, among other awards, the Honor Award of the Commercial Development Association and the Adhesive & Sealant Council Award in 1982. He is a Trustee of Johns Hopkins University, and a member of several professional organizations.

PETER F. McCLOSKEY

President, Electronic Industries Association. Mr. McCloskey oversees the activities of the national trade organization that represents U.S. manufacturers in the electronics industry, whose products range from the smallest components to the most complex systems used by defense, space and industry. Previously, he was President of the Computer and Business Equipment Manufacturers Association. Mr. McCloskey was President and Chairman of the Board of Farrington Manufacturing Company, has held various management positions with International Business Machines Corporation, and was in private law practice.

JAMES W. McKEE, JR.

Chairman and Chief Executive Officer, CPC International, Inc. Mr. McKee joined the international division of CPC International in 1947, and served with the company's affiliates in Italy and Brazil. He was Managing Director of Refinacoes de Milho, the oldest and one of the largest CPC Latin American affiliates. After several positions in top management, he became President and Chief Administrative Officer of CPC in 1969, and Chief Executive Officer three years later. He was elected Chairman in 1979, with continuing responsibility as CEO. In recognition of his contributions to that country, the Brazilian government awarded Mr. McKee the Cruzeiro do Sul (Southern Cross). Mr. McKee is a Trustee and Co-Chairman of The Conference Board, Inc.

EGILS MILBERGS

Director of the Office of Productivity, Technology and Innovation, U.S. Department of Commerce. Prior to his appointment, Mr. Milbergs served as policy adviser on business regulations for the Reagan transition team. The purpose of OPTI is to assist in stimulating private productivity improvement through development of relevant public policies, cooperative R&D arrangements, and the provision of productivity-related information and technical assistance. Mr. Milbergs was previously at SRI International, where he managed research in science and technology policy, commercialization of federally funded R&D, technology transfer to developing countries, as well as serving as a strategic planning consultant to major companies. He has also served as a policy analyst with the Office of Management and Budget and was assigned to the President's Advisory Council on Executive Organization (Ash Council).

EDWARD B. ROBERTS

David Sarnoff Professor of the Management of Technology and Chairman of the MIT Technology and Health Management Group, MIT Sloan School of Management. Dr. Roberts has been engaged in developing and applying analytical approaches to the organization and management of research and development and health-care delivery since 1958. He co-founded the MIT Research Program on the Management of Science and Technology, an area he presently leads. Previously, he co-founded what is now the MIT System Dynamics Research Program.

DAVID S. SAXON

President, University of California, at the time of this conference, Dr. Saxon is now Chairman of the Corporation of the Massachusetts Institute of Technology. At Berkeley, he was earlier a Professor, Dean of Physical Sciences, Vice Chancellor and Executive Vice Chancellor. He also served as a physicist at the National Bureau of Standards. He was recently Visiting Fellow at Merton College, Oxford University. Dr. Saxon is a member of several professional associations.

ROLAND W. SCHMITT

Senior Vice President, Corporate Research and Development, General Electric Company. Dr. Schmitt held several R&D management positions before becoming Vice President, Corporation R&D, in 1978, and Senior Vice President in 1982. He is on the Governing Board of the American Institute of Physics, and is a Director of the Industrial Research Institute. Dr. Schmitt is a Fellow of the American Physical Society, Institute of Electrical and Electronics Engineers, and the American Association for the Advancement of Science, and a member of the National Academy of Engineering and the National Science Board. Vice Chairman of the Board of the New York State Science and Technology Foundation, and Chairman of the Investment Review Committee of its Corporation for Innovation Development, he is a Trustee of Rensselaer Polytechnic Institute.

LEO J. THOMAS

Senior Vice President and Director of the Kodak Research Laboratories. Dr. Thomas joined Kodak as a research chemist in the color photography division of the Research Laboratories. He served in several management positions until named Director of the Research Laboratories in 1977, and Senior Vice President the following year. He is a Director of the Industrial Research Institute, New York State Science and Technology Foundation, and High Technology of Rochester, Inc., and serves as a Trustee of the Rochester Museum and Science Center. Dr. Thomas is a member of the Research and Development Council of the American Management Associations, and a member of several professional oganizations.

T.L. TOLBERT

Director, External Research and Development, Monsanto Company. Dr. Tolbert holds oversight responsibility for all of Monsanto's university and other external research programs. He joined the Chemstrand Corporation, a Monsanto subsidiary, as an organic chemist. He was later transferred to Monsanto's Corporate Research Laboratories, where he held a variety of assignments in research and technology management prior to assuming his current responsibilities. Member of several professional associations, Dr. Tolbert is active on committees of the Council for Chemical Research, a consortium that brings together participants from university chemical and chemical engineering departments and the chemical industry.

ROBERT E. WILSON

Senior Vice President and Director, Heidrick and Struggles. Dr. Wilson has been responsible for identifying chief technical officers for several major companies. He worked in research and development at Corn Products Company before joining the University of Dayton as Professor and Head of the Department of Chemical Engineering. In addition to technical consulting with the U.S. Navy, Air Force, and private industry during this period, he formed and directed the University of Dayton's College of Engineering Graduate Program. Returning to industry, he was Director of Process Development/Engineering for Thomas J. Lipton, Inc., then joined International Minerals and Chemical Company, as Director of R&D, prior to his present post.

Why This Report

As U.S. industry has been afflicted by prolonged recession at home and abroad and mounting competition from other industrial nations, notably Japan, there has been a renaissance of interest in research and development. Recent developments in such fields as biotechnology, computers and materials science suggest that R&D holds great promise for restoring U.S. preeminence in the world marketplace. Adroit management of the R&D function will be necessary, however, if that promise is to be fulfilled.

Earlier this year The Conference Board organized a conference at which leading experts in R&D management shared their experiences and ideas with each other and with other interested representatives of corporate and technical management. Because of the high caliber of the presentations on that occasion, they have been edited for publication, as have the question-and-answer exchanges among the session chairmen, the speakers, and the audience.

On behalf of The Conference Board, I offer thanks to the six chairmen and eighteen speakers who made the Conference—and, I trust, this volume—so useful. Their names are appropriately listed within.

JAMES T. MILLS
President

Part I

An Overview
Chairman: Robert A. Charpie
President
Cabot Corporation

Chapter 1
R&D Complexity and Competition

W.O. Baker
Chairman, Rockefeller University
Retired Chairman of the Board
Bell Laboratories

"R&D: complexity and competition" says what every businessman knows: that it's necessary to get there first, with the best, but there is really no way to do it. That "impossibility," of course, has always been a good stimulus for research and development. But research and development are changing dramatically. Worldwide, science is steadily infusing industrial research and development. This is happening so fully that the classic single invention, discovery of the startling new molecule, and even the ingenious secret subsystem, will be increasingly rare, because the vast common scientific and technical knowledge base is increasingly available to everyone everywhere.

The game, then, is how good an environment we can generate to keep our economic and industrial security strengths, without disillusioning our managers and investors about what can be expected from industrial laboratories. But that means that we must mobilize capabilities—which, indeed, the nation has—and use them wisely. These needs encompass primarily a better knowledge base, a better way of organizing knowledge for action so that, in the remainder of the 20th century, we can properly apply the scientific and technical information that has been doubling in recorded form about every seven years since 1950. Until these recent years, it has been quite possible for a given industry—whether steel, rubber, pharmaceuticals, electronics or automobiles—to make technical, and hence operational, decisions on the basis of references contained in its own technology. Automobile makers knew about their power trains and engine hookups, and could adjust engineering to style and driveability considerations with a relatively contained set of options. Now the electronics and dynamics of fuel injection, emission control, and the like require these engineering decisions to be linked to a large domain of science and engineering, such as solid-state science and chemical catalysis. Similarly, the metal shaper and machine fabricator earlier could concentrate on the science and engineering of metallurgy, but now they have to balance the design and economic considerations with those of plastics and other composites, which are, in turn, supported by a vast science of polymers and their macromolecular basis.

But these are only the broad contours of the changes we are facing. Thus we had better think some more about the parts of civilization that have concentrated on the organization of broad knowledge systems—chiefly universities and colleges. We also had better think hard about how to get machine aids and other help in communicating to overall management and R&D leaders as to opportunities and requirements of commercial survival and progress. Technically, these are coming to be less matters of familiar domestic competition and more those of world science expansion. This introduces new complexity to the selection and pursuit of appropriate R&D. Indeed, the very volume of scientific activity has injected a new complexity into all development and engineering, whether industrial or governmental. For attending this epochal expansion of scientific work has been a growing evidence that the scope of new knowledge about matter, energy and organisms is now such that it will almost always find some application, and that some development will be stimulated. This is a new condition. For a thousand years scientific knowledge was often accumulated to form a precious increase in understanding, without necessarily having much relation to application. A new principle—"if you know it, you are likely to use it"—is taking hold. Since knowledge is getting to be worldwide, our traditional, rational, orderly evaluation of industrial technology, which pays suitable attention to existing investment in established production cultures, including required labor practices, financing routines, and the like, is in for larger and larger revisions. Various other nations just do not operate in our way.

But also in the face of this change, obviously competing technologies will *not* necessarily be attached to competing products, as they usually have been in the Western world. (The old habit of doing what your competitor does, only just a little cheaper or better—and devoting a good bit of science and engineering to product differentiation rather than product change—are comforts we are going to lose.)

R&D Funding

We should also remind ourselves of the scale on which industrial R&D is already being conducted, and hence of why we really must think deeply about managing it for the interest of the firm, the public, and the nation. Thus, in 1982, of over $75 billion that was spent in total in the nation for R&D, companies' funding for research and development was about $37 billion. Over half of the total federal R&D spending is contracted to industry. Thus there are strong links of industrial R&D management to federal policies and public purposes. Yet we have learned that "spillover" or "fallout" into commercial resources and competency from the federal funding of space and defense is mostly myth. This is reflected in our complaints about competing nations not carrying defense burdens, and outstripping us in industrial high technology as well as conventional fields. As we all know, our vast and necessary defense performance in industry has not protected or even aided us in this other realm.

In 1983, about 800 companies will spend about $38 billion of their own funds, and roughly $20 billion of federal funds, to do about $58 to $60 billion of the science technology and engineering of the United States. Top corporate managements have kept up their allotments to independent research and development in the face of falling profits. Further, on the average, in these 800 companies about 40 percent of after-tax profits are put into this investment for the future. Accordingly, R&D financing is already prominent in industrial management and policy. But there are great variations among industries. For instance, the largest R&D investment is by the automobile industry; the eighth and ninth largest by the petrochemicals and fuels industries, respectively, where there is a total industry investment of about $2.5 billion per year. Machinery and machine tools R&D, spread among a large number of companies, spends a total of about half a billion dollars, amounting still to about 36 percent of profits. Metals and mining, with about the same total sales, spends about half that

much—$250 million, or about 22 percent of profits. In steel, about $180 million of R&D spending is about 11 percent of profits.[1]

Is there some logical or consistent strategy that determines these figures? Is there something about the science and technology underlying the work in these industries that causes fourfold or larger variations in allocation of funds, as a proportion of profits, to research and development? Further, is this range of investment for the future being suitably evaluated so as to assure ability in international competiton? What should be the relative weighting of public policy about technical strength of these basic industries, with respect to national security? (Perhaps at a given profit level, R&D supplements should be sought.) Studies for the Federal Emergency Management Agency indicate a severe lag in capability to respond for a national defense output. At the same time, we are allocating huge funds to development of public systems which would have to be manufactured from the materials and processes that these severely stressed companies provide.

All this underscores the magnitude of R&D management's responsibilities. They reach into strategic arenas; they link the public and private purposes; and they must pursue goals on a scale previously considered to be too large for scientists and engineers. And this is happening at a time when the actual content of science and engineering is of unprecedented complexity, and is being subjected to global competition. These responsibilities extend into bold and drastic revisions of cooperation and coordination of international trade, competitive machinery such as the patenting and proprietorship of software, publications and regulatory processes. There remain as well the obvious and familiar ones of tax mechanisms, credit programs, and, above all, human resources and education. Obviously, the kind of competition now pressing on all of U.S. industry, and the complication of industrial R&D requiring ever-closer links with these general management issues, call for improved organizing and managing.

More Use of Systems Engineering

One aspect of this is a wider use of systems engineering. Many derivatives of this information-handling and operations-management scheme and technology have arisen. Modern operations research is one aspect that was strongly applied during World War II. Improved statistical analysis is another contributor. The largest current impetus comes from expanding

[1]National Science Foundation, *Science Resources Studies Highlights,* NSF 82-324, NSF 82-325, and NSF 82-329; "R&D Scoreboard: Research Spending Defies Recession." *Business Week,* July 5, 1982.

computer modeling and simulation of new technology and its result in systems. And certain aspects of the "artificial intelligence" theme have been based on these extensions of systems engineering. Particularly appealing examples, now often called "expert systems research," involve medical diagnostic and therapeutic machine aids, such as the MYCIN system at Stanford, for the application of antibiotics in cases of intense human infection.[2]

The useful application of systems engineering and systems analysis to the management of research and development involves combining extensive knowledge bases in the underlying physical (and, increasingly, biological) sciences with overlays of economics and, even, policy aspects of labor, environment and other human-resource parameters. It appears, however, that the emerging dependencies of industrial R&D on such overlays are now so vivid that management requires more general application of systems principles. For applying basic science, suitable systems concepts require scales of technical range and utility, such as the frequency span of the electromagnetic spectrum for industries of communications, computer, information handling, signaling and control sensors, and the like. In finer detail, often empirical statements of efficiencies, such as the kind of transmission medium suitable for given band widths of signals, or circuits suitable for particular logic or memory systems, have been effective. Such relationships need to be developed for analogous matters such as power-train functions in automotive vehicles, and other variables of propulsion which extend the understanding of options outside of the present (roughly 17 percent) efficiency of energy conversion from the engine to the wheel on the road.

In the dynamic areas of biomedicine, pharmaceuticals and health care, a similar plot of pharmacodynamic qualities of various therapeutic agents is needed. Thus, on the basis that whatever medicine the patient takes won't do much unless it gets somewhere, one would expect the systems engineering of these agents to show diffusion and transport qualities of various significant families of molecules. This could involve both intra- and extra-cellular functions.

In the basic systems operations for materials synthesis and processing, appropriate phase diagrams and generalized strength and fatigue relationships would be helpful. The basic physical property characterization of the system appropriately linked, in the case of chemical and metallurgical processes, to overall kinetic parameters would provide an increasingly valuable reference scale for that part of the systems-engineering exercise.

R&D Linkages

Even more compelling, however, will be the relationship of these conventional engineering science qualities to the kinds of decisions about industrial R&D that are related to public policy, market economics, corporate culture, and the specific financial and working conditions of particular enterprises. Before suggesting the demanding task of integrating these crucial relationships closely with R&D management, I cite a few background items.

• It now takes about nine years after discovery of a new drug for it to be approved for use in the United States. Licensing and review of new power plants may take longer.

• Worldwide, our dependence on overseas use of all products is dominated by an unfavorable U.S. trade balance of about \$35 billion in such vital commodities as steel, automobiles and machine tools. In 1960, our total dependence on international trade was less than 10 percent of Gross National Product; last year it was more than 25 percent of GNP.[3]

• France, Japan and West Germany each devotes 10 to 15 percent of government-supported R&D to industrial application. The United States devotes less than 1 percent to this purpose.

• Our defense and space R&D funding is \$30 billion, 50 percent more than that of Japan, West Germany and France put together.

• Our intrinsic industrial spending for R&D is of about the same magnitude as the total spent for industry by *both* government and privately in Japan, France and West Germany.

These loosely connected items have tightly felt impacts on future industrial research and development. But what about some rationalizing factor, such as the magic of economics, that ought to bring together the external forces, allowing commercial and social forces to be assessed neatly against our knowledge of energy and matter, particles and waves, which constitute all the real parts of the universe? This matter of how the R&D director can merge modern economics and model building with computers into an ingenious strategy for competition in complex phenomena is one of the most intriguing questions of all. An exercise in the relationship was attempted by Dr. Hannay, from our Laboratories, and Dr. Landau of Halcon, a couple of years ago in a volume of essays by technologists and economists, *Taxation, Technology and the U.S. Economy* (Pergamon

---

[2]R.O. Duda and E.H. Shortlifbi, "Expert Systems Research." *Science,* April 15, 1983, p. 261.

[3]"America's Competitive Challenge: The Need for a National Response." Report to the President from Business/Higher Education Forum, April, 1983.

Press, 1981). (This was at least a more sophisticated assembly than the analysis attempted by Dr. Milton Harris and myself some years before, on behalf of the American Chemical Society. In our paper, entitled "Chemistry and the Economy," we made no serious attempt to satisfy experts in economics but rather adapted their principles to our amateurish expectations.)

Subsequently, Dr. Landau wrote a monograph for the National Academy of Engineering which appeared late in 1982 under the title *Technology, Economics and Politics,* and was subtitled *Observations of an Entrepreneur.* This essay is a kind of purging of conscience by Landau. It has a lot of fascinating personal views, but deep within the lively text are some prime truths. One that puts it all together is: "There is no real provision, accordingly, for the entrepreneur and technological innovation in economic theory." This was not exactly what we had in mind when we founded a research department of economics in our Laboratories some years ago, but I now confess that we founded it in the absence of any professional economist. The distinguished ones we have acquired in the years since seemed relieved and even exhilarated that industrial R&D and its systems engineering adducts were finally cheerfully groping for new economic insights. We were undaunted by the inapplicability of conventional economics, which nevertheless was supposed to represent the vital processes of the rest of the operations of the firm. It is indeed a curious situation that industrial R&D and innovation are supposed to be the major elements in economic growth, but have not yet been adequately accounted for in corporate economics.

Accumulating and Organizing Information

Reminded of these unnerving instances of the knowledge, or even guesswork, that must be integrated with the behavior of atoms and molecules to establish the kind of systems engineering that may be valuable for industrial R&D, let us look further at ways in which to organize knowledge for action. The usual one is the accumulating record of information about science and engineering in print, microfiche and, increasingly, digital tapes, optical discs, and other modern records. The volume of such information has now reached a level where it is frequently dealt with by ignoring it. Especially bypassed is action on the increased data in many languages, and their storage in the recondite recesses of bibliography. "It's easier to do it over than to look it up," some say.

This doctrine overlooks the probability that you almost certainly will not get it right the first time over. More significantly, it omits the crucial and invaluable role of the organization of knowledge that does inhabit the literature, despite what a frustrated browser may think.

Many a technical writer has used a career-long experience to put each item of discovery and interpretation into a wider context in the field. These efforts, properly covered, can aid the research and development program director to assess the promise and posture of fields being considered for commercial development.

But laboratory leaders and those working wth overall corporate management must refine and organize this vast knowledge base so that it is ever closer to R&D plans and programs, ever more readily accessible to the individual scientists and engineers who will ultimately carry out those programs. Recording and distributing knowledge are curiously erratic processes in our nation. During the late 1950's and early 1960's, when national security was challenged by overseas capabilities, I instituted and organized a variety of unprecedented systems for bibliography and information handling in science and technology through the White House Science Office, the Federal Council of Science and Technology, and the Science Information Council. This domain became known as STI, Science and Technology Information. Much of that structure has vanished, just as the actual volume of new information has surged. But the policies we promoted then also emphasized the role of independent, nongovernmental bibliographic and information-handling capabilities. Accordingly, the professional societies—the American Chemical Society, for example, through the Chemical Abstract System, and many others—have moved forward with skill and enterprise. Nevertheless, we must now renew efforts to meet the responsibilities, such as those given to the National Science Foundation 25 years ago, to foster STI. A review session by the American Federation of Indexing and Abstracting Societies in 1982 demonstrated that we are seriously lagging. This time around, we must go further than before, and recognize the enormous potentials of machine organization of information while at the same time preserving and applying the remarkable human ability to integrate and interpret.

I turn now to a role of universities, and call attention to the 14th Annual Report of the National Science Board for 1983, *University-Industry Research Relationships: Myths, Realities and Potentials.* This is a lively and expert account of how industrial R&D is seeking more and more university participation. But it wisely notes that industrial sponsors do not expect to get major new ideas from these programs, although, of course, they will augment the utterly vital acquisition of human talent. The report points out: "Contrary to some expectations, innovation is not a major industrial motivation for university/industry interactions. Industry rarely looks to the university for technological innovations that result directly in new products or processes. Universities often perceive themselves as idea generators, but if a company must go outside its own organization for such innovations it is unlikely to go to a university." The report discusses a whole variety of pertinent factors in the present and future of industrial competition and R&D, but it is practically silent on the compelling point that universities are where knowledge is organized and conveyed most extensively. Therefore, they should foster this systematic accumulation of technology-stimulating information.

Curiously, the most practical and commercial R&D functions are aided by systems engineering, whose complex interfaces between science and society depend heavily on this knowledge base at universities. Yet the original academic inputs are often said to shape new knowledge in the most impractical ways. It appears that the very points that the National Science Board Report properly identifies, particularly in the section "Trends and Opportunities," as most challenging for industrial progress through scientific and technical strengths are ones that demand better organization of literature and its use. But the report has no emphasis on scientific and technical information resources.

A more organized view of the values of others' work can be among the many useful derivatives of STI practice, recast by the modern use of digital processors. This can support a keener management perception of what technology and science are saying and doing throughout the world. Incidentally, a study reported early in 1982 by King Research, Inc., for the Department of Energy estimated that 60,000 scientists and engineers, nationally supported by the $6 billion annual research and development budget of that Department, read about 7.1 million journal articles and 6.6 million technical reports yearly. The study went on to make one of the usual operational estimates, which by the way do have a valuable systems-engineering implication, that the R&D program saves about $13 billion annually as a result of this literature knowledge input and stimulation. It is believed that about $6 billion is required worldwide to generate and organize the information involved, so this sort of estimated return is indeed industrially appealing.[4] But the future potential inputs from such use and extension of the knowledge base can go much beyond even these value scales.

A report to the Engineers Joint Council dwelt on computers as aids in human decision making and noted "engineering, education, and research should draw attention to the role of computers as accessories to human judgment in deciding about complex, often technical situations." The report concluded with many specific suggestions about the computer design and

operations systems that seem to bear closely on the issues facing us today. The main trouble with the report is that it was published on May 26, 1962, in a volume entitled *The Nation's Engineering Research Needs, 1965-1985*, (W.O. Baker, "Information Handling Systems," p. 153). While we still have two years until 1985, we have not yet adequately met a major share of the expectations laid out in this study. We have made several passes and have had some near misses at appropriate nationwide federal support for this work in universities and other centers.

A more recent volume, *What Can Be Automated,*[5] picks up many of the scientific and technical questions raised in 1962, and shows that understanding of some computing principles has been enhanced just as the machine and hardware capability have leaped forward. However, the crucial issues of software applications have lagged seriously. Some experience, however, can be submitted. Thus, in the early 1960's at Bell Labs, we began intensively to generate a series of automated operations in telecommunications and also in related equipment manufacture and design, which we have called "operations support systems," and which have been designated in various annual statements and policy discussions by top corporate management as "The Acronym Revolution." These are now widespread, as specific adjuncts to our development programs, and the innovation of systems in production and use. More than 150 of them have been credited with keeping productivity moving at an annual rate of about 7 percent, even under conditions where the national average of gain in productivity was said to be zero or negative.

We believe that these very specific and detailed process automata, whose software production has often led us to a completely new understanding of the things we were doing in telecommunications for generations, have even more widespread potentials for machine building, service industries, all types of consumer product fabrication, and the like. They should, however, be conceived and applied in the advanced or final stage of development at the latest, and well before a new product is hurriedly consigned to be made in a conventional or old plant. Fortunately, the hardware support for these systems is increasingly provided by economical minicomputers or assemblies of microprocessors.

One of the conclusions of the 1962 EJC report will serve to summarize those observations on R&D complexity and competition. "Since the domain of the engineer is no smaller than that of human activity, we end, as we began, on a theme of how, through the organization of technical information, man's use of logical machines can magnify his works."

[4]King Research, Inc., *The Value of the Energy Data Base*, DOE/OR/11232-1. Washington, D.C.: Department of Energy, 1982.

[5]B. Arden, ed., *What Can Be Automated*. Cambridge, Mass.: MIT Press, 1980.

Part II
Top Management Looks at R&D

Chairman: Robert A. Charpie
President
Cabot Corporation

Chapter 2
R&D: The Major Risks

J.E. Goldman
Retired Senior Vice President and Chief Scientist
Xerox Corporation

R&D is a "black box" to top management. The computer analogy may be a very appropriate one. Like computers, the black box of R&D has input ports, output ports, and perhaps a few feedback loops and peripherals tied onto it. Constituted as it is by lawyers, salesmen and bean counters, top management is usually not conversant with the inner workings of the black box. It looks to the output: the impact on the product line, or the processes that make the product. It has a notion that there is probably a linear relationship between the output and the input (the personnel and resources that are committed by the enterprise). Since those resources are a drain on earnings, top management would love to see an amplification factor introduced so that input is minimized while output is optimized. Thus, it expects that R&D will enhance the profitability of the corporate enterprise. There are inherent risks in each of the elements of the R&D black box.

People and Resources

Regarding people, dedication to excellence on the part of the institution and on the part of the R&D enterprise is probably the most serious and most important commitment of all. Here is the first risk faced by top management. It is customary simply to look at the marketplace, look at the statistics and the data on salaries and other forms of remuneration provided by the various external sources. Instead, the approach should be to concentrate on the quality of people recruited and the assignments given them; costs should be left until later.

I know this approach may escalate a rate of compensation that has already escalated beyond what has been anticipated by managers—particularly financial managers. But since people are the most important

ingredient in the R&D enterprise and, therefore, its most important risk, in putting together the R&D enterprise, sustaining it, and continually evaluating it, one must be certain of having the best people. Mediocrity has never resulted in successful R&D.

R&D is a game. (I recommend Dave Allison's well-known book, *The R&D Game.*[1]) R&D should be played like poker, a game for which I have an affinity. When another player has an exposed pair of aces, you don't stick around with a pair of deuces.

The end purpose of R&D is both defensive and offensive in terms of the strategies of the company: defensive in the sense of forestalling technological obsolescence, and offensive in the sense of gaining competitive advantage through improvement of existing product or development of attractive new products. The only way to play the R&D game, to survive and succeed in the competitive environment, is to ensure that the quality of the company's R&D people at least measures up to—and preferably exceeds—that of counterparts in competitive organizations. Of course, it is the recruiting process that yields the cards for the R&D game.

A parenthetical comment is in order. One of the great assets of R&D—more of R than of D—to the corporate enterprise, an asset not often recognized by management, is the utilization of R&D people as a calibration for the rest of the organization. R&D scientists inevitably interact with the outside world. They are probably the only constituency within the corporation which draws its life's blood from its interaction with an outside (scientific) community. The same is true, though to less extent, of

[1]David Allison, *The R&D Game.* Cambridge, Mass.: MIT Press, 1969.

engineers, who interact with their colleagues in the outside world. By and large, the rest of the organization does not. If the assessment of the company's R&D people by the outside scientific and engineering communities is high, that can raise the level of performance by the rest of the company.

The next element of input for the R&D black box is resources. How does an organization commit its resources to R&D?

The conventional wisdom in the corporate executive suite is to study the *Fortune* 500 list, or the *Business Week* annual report on R&D, and determine what competitors do. What percentage of their revenues are spent on R&D, or, if one elects to use Bill Baker's norm, what percentage of profits? (See page 2.) Parenthetically, in some high-technology companies, the commitment to R&D can even exceed the profits of the company; and, in many instances, *should* exceed the profits of the company, if the corporation is to grow significantly.

I think that competitive R&D expenditures are a poor way to determine how much to spend on R&D, but the appropriate amount of expenditure is a question to which I really don't have answers. Having played the R&D game for most of my professional life, on many occasions I would approach management and say: "Look, we must have this; we must have that." Yet sometimes, sitting on the other side of the table and looking at how the corporation commits its resources as a whole, I felt ambiguous about the question because, as a member of management, I had to have my eye on the bottom line.

But the nature of a commitment can often be as important as its magnitude. The reason is very simple and straightforward. Top management recognizes output. The positive feedback loop from output to input is not hard to track, nor difficult to understand. The positive feedback of a good result—a new product, a new process, an improvement, a cost-cutting mechanism—is readily comprehended. The only problem is time: It may take five to twenty years. If it is accomplished in five years, that is a very good result. But negative feedback is very, very quick—it is virtually instantaneous. If something is done to disrupt the community of scholars that constitutes the R&D enterprise, it is felt immediately. It is felt in their morale, in their corporate loyalty; ultimately it is translated into loss of productivity. After all, it is productivity that we endeavor to manage and to measure in an R&D establishment.

How should the input resources be committed? I am mindful of an experience, years ago, when I was directing the scientific research laboratory of The Ford Motor Company. Henry Ford II was being very progressive when he suggested: Let us not, in our company, measure the output of research year to year. Rather let us assure a five-year stable budget for the research enterprise, and we'll look at it at the end of five years.

Stability and continuity are, perhaps, the most important ingredients in R&D: Their absence constitutes a risk for top management.

Processor Risks

Now we move into the processor itself, that black box. As I have observed, top management really has little idea of what goes on inside that black box and less of an idea on how to manage it. This is where the responsibility of R&D management lies, for it understands what happens in the black box and what needs to be changed.

Top management must place faith in the R&D management to optimize the productivity of the R&D establishment and produce output useful to the company. The "processor" risk for top management, then, is to choose competent R&D managers, and then let them do their jobs.

Output Risks

What is output? Put together a fine R&D establishment: It will produce papers that are published; it will produce new products; it will improve processes and existing products. With luck, the output will feed back very quickly—or feed forward, really, into the rest of the corporation.

How the corporation utilizes output is, in my judgment, the R&D risk that top management takes. The risk has several manifestations. One is rigid insistence on relevance. If an R&D establishment has first-class people, geniuses at work, some of this output is likely to transcend the immediate requirements and needs of the corporation—to have no apparent business possibilities. But if top management denigrates this output, castigates those responsible for it, the company will be in trouble. First of all, outstanding scientists will not permit themselves to be constrained intellectually. Second, no one can recognize today what will be relevant tomorrow. The myriad possibilities of how technology might affect the company's product lines, the new markets it might enter, urgently bespeak open-mindedness by top management and its bestowal of freedom on technical people to go into directions that *they* feel are relevant. This is not to suggest that top management should give carte blanche to the pursuit of irrelevancies, but that it must allow for diffusion by R&D people into analogous and neighboring fields of study.

To illustrate: The research laboratory at Ford was the sole voice in the wilderness which was crying out in the early 1960's that there would be an energy shortage some day, and that, when it came, Ford cars and trucks should be much more energy efficient than they then were. No one else in the company paid heed. It is from the research enterprise that Cassandra-like or millenarian voices are raised. They are not likely to be raised by the financial executive, by the sales executive, by the production executive, by anyone concerned with sales performance in the next ten days.

When R&D output *is* relevant, another risk arises for top management. The question is: How can the output be effectively and efficiently plugged into the system, particularly if the researchers are outpacing the perceptions and conventional wisdom of the marketplace, which is not "ready" for new technology that sooner or later will inevitably be adopted. The risk is that top management will dally, will fritter away the competitive advantage that adoption of the new technology today would give it.

I submit another personal experience. In the late 1950's, the market researchers who analyzed the potential demand for copying machines suggested that the total market in the world would be about 5,000 machines. That was not instructive or useful to the researchers who were trying to produce a radically different machine relying on the principles of xerography, which they hoped would make the reproduction of documents much easier and more inexpensive, and, therefore, much more widespread than it ever had been. Fortunately, top management bet on the researchers, not on the market researchers.

The final risk I shall discuss is top management's assessment of R&D output that transcends the present product line of the company, but seems commercially plausible. If efforts are not made to get this output into the marketplace, the R&D people will be frustrated and money will have been wasted. But if efforts are to be made, choosing the right course to pursue will be difficult, and will be attended by risk. I believe that one of the most important ingredients of progressive management in an enterprise that has strong and effective R&D is to make sound provision for utilizing those results of R&D that may not fit precisely with the present business of the corporation.

The solutions can take a variety of forms. It may take the form of an internal venture management group. It may take the form of a spin-off. It may take the form of backing, and encouraging local banks or venture capitalists to back, a colleague who wants to leave the company and start an enterprise that will exploit offbeat discoveries in the laboratory. Through such vehicles, large corporations can capitalize on the talent and imagination of their capable R&D staffs when that talent and imagination yield an idea that, properly nourished, will generate a vigorous new business tomorrow. If a company does not exploit such opportunities, its R&D organization and the mainstream output of that organization will suffer.

Chapter 3
When the Pendulum Should Swing Toward More Basic Research

Robert H. Krieble
Chairman and Chief Executive Officer
Loctite Corporation

"When the Pendulum Should Swing Toward More Basic Research" is an intriguing topic which Loctite has addressed. We do not propose that our approach provides the best, or only, answers but it appears to have worked reasonably well for us.

About Loctite

Loctite is an international company involved in the development, manufacture and sales of specialty adhesives, sealants and maintenance products to the industrial original equipment manufacturer, maintenance and repair, consumer and automotive aftermarket markets. Worldwide, we employ 2,500 people and our annual sales run to about $200 million. We consider ourselves to be a high-technology company, and rely heavily on our ability to match our technical capabilities with customers' identified needs. About 10 percent of our people are involved in the technical area.

Our product range includes adhesives for locking threaded fasteners, bonding shaft parts (such as bushings, sleeves, bearings and gears), liquid gasketing materials, structural adhesives, instant-setting cyanoacrylate adhesives, and adhesive coatings and potting compounds cured with ultraviolet light. In the consumer and automotive aftermarket area, we employ a considerable range of different chemistries as the foundation for a range of over 150 different products. These chemistries include anaerobic, epoxy, cyanoacrylate, silicone, polyester, daylight curing methacrylates, modified acrylic, plastisol, alkyd resin, and protective coating technologies. The breadth of our chemical skills is matched in many ways by our statement of the company mission: "Loctite will be the no. 1 market share seller of high value, branded chemical products that help our customers assemble, seal, repair and maintain the things they own or make."

Loctite has three main R&D centers; one in Newington, Connecticut; one just outside Cleveland, Ohio; and one in Dublin, Ireland. We believe strongly in the benefits of a close relationship between the R&D laboratory and the marketplace.

How Loctite Views R&D

At Loctite, we consider five major roles for the R&D and commercial development functions:

(1) basic research;
(2) product development;
(3) process development;
(4) application development;
(5) commercial development.

Today we are really dealing with the question of the balance between the first, basic research, and the other four.

We split our thinking into *basic chemistry* and *applied chemistry*. We define *basic* as the search for new properties through the generation of unique chemistry, or the use of known chemistry modified to be compatible with Loctite's needs. *Applied* chemistry we define as the development of specific products to meet identified customer application needs by formulation. We regard very highly the role of expert formulation and see it as a key ingredient in our success.

To get to the key question of this section—How much basic? how much applied?—I would like to present an analogy. We like to think of our range of chemical capabilities as library books. We use these books, as it were, to show us how to formulate new, or modify current, products to meet identified needs. In the main, the motivation for basic work is generated by apparent gaps in our library of chemical capabilities. Basic programs are initiated and funded to generate the necessary new chemistry to allow these capabilities to be put into our library for use by our new product-development activities.

With this approach, the problem becomes how to decide when our library is inadequate to serve our needs. The solution emerges from a very close relationship among application development, product development, and basic research, working in a continuous feedback loop. A very important aspect of this loop is management's perception of the balance maintained between the continuous stream of new application requirements with available chemistry.

This area clearly calls for judgment with regard to the limitations of technology and the difference between possible and impossible requirements. As a rule, therefore, our basic programs are aimed at correcting major deficiencies in our ability to meet new needs.

The actual question of how much basic research should be done is almost impossible to answer generally: It will vary from company to company. If a company is continuously finding more and more application opportunities in the marketplace that it cannot service due to lack of technical ability to meet application requirements, then this is a good barometer that more basic work is warranted, or that an outside search for additional technology must be initiated in order to acquire the needed capability. As a very general rule, Loctite would visualize that somewhere between 10 and 20 percent of the R&D budget should be devoted to the generation and understanding of fundamental technology necessary to formulate products meeting required performance profiles.

The alternative to swinging the pendulum toward more basic work is to try to run harder and harder to meet the field needs with chemistry and/or technology that is at or close to the limits of its capabilities. This approach can be very detrimental on many fronts. In the first instance, it causes conflict between R&D and marketing, since major compromises are more and more frequently required. Marketing sees R&D as losing its creative ability, and R&D accuses marketing of always asking for the impossible. R&D morale begins to suffer seriously as it begins to see the clear limitations of its ability to produce significant results. Since R&D productivity does, in fact, begin to slip—and successful projects become more infrequent—people spend more and more time trying to justify failure, rather than quickly moving ahead and simply accepting failure as part of R&D progress.

Two Case Studies

Loctite started with a unique chemistry, looking for applications of the so-called anaerobic adhesives. It was a slow and tedious process trying to convince the engineering community that it could quite effectively replace mechanical means with a few drops of a chemical and, by so doing, produce a better product at a lower cost.

For the first 12 years or so we had no chemistry limitations. Our problem was credibility with each new application. We certainly had ample technology to do the job; the problem was convincing people, that is to say, the sales force and our customers. However, after about 12 years, when we had made considerable inroads into the mechanical threadlocking market, our original target market, we began to find more and more new applications, like bearings for tension, and the potential of replacing standard gaskets with liquid products.

The latter held out great potential, since one tube of a liquid gasketing product could, in theory, eliminate the problem of stocking a vast range of different cut gaskets. Our problem was that the original threadlocking chemistry was not directly suitable for either the retaining or the gasketing area. This was probably our first experience in starting a more fundamental program to generate new properties by the synthesis of new prepolymer materials, permitting us to build greater adhesive properties and flexibility into the same molecule. (Our original methacrylate systems were hard, brittle materials with very little adhesion.)

Another early decision to move into fundamental work related to the function of surfaces in the cure chemistry of our systems. Loctite products were very active liquid formulations that remained liquid when exposed to the oxygen in the air, but quickly changed into the solid state when air was excluded and the liquid was in contact with an iron surface. Hence the early threadlocking orientation—iron surfaces and the liquid being confined between the nut and the bolt with air being excluded.

Soon applications using stainless steel and plated surfaces appeared, and our early products had serious problems. Programs were funded to study the exact nature of our curing chemistry, with a view to developing chemistry that would work equally well on surfaces other than iron.

Some General Observations

With the reduced level of support for research by governments, we feel that closer ties among academic institutions would be desirable and probably very productive. We do not see that industry has any direct responsibility in this, but would probably do well to recognize the likelihood that overall research funding is likely to suffer. Loctite has some fine relationships with local academic institutions and several in Europe where this type of industrial-academic relationship appears to be fostered with great enthusiasm.

Of course, research does not follow a neat tidy path to the initial objective. It is a difficult area to measure in terms of productivity. Indeed, sometimes it is even difficult to know what the results are, and to judge their importance. Some faith in the research process is required. It needs long-term commitment since it will suffer greatly from stop-and-go tactics. It is important to recognize the risks. Certainly, the original objectives will not always be achieved, but a company cannot stand still either. New and better ways to do things will be found, and we like to feel that we have a good chance of being the one to find them.

R&D people are always the first to recognize the lack of chemistry or technology, but are not always the first to highlight it as a major company problem; hence the need for continuous involvement of top management in the R&D-marketing process. There must be a willingness to accept the fact that technology does reach limits, and that "new" is often better than more of the same.

In Loctite, we have tried very hard to achieve constant interaction between top management and our R&D people. We rely heavily on what we call our Technology Planning Board, which provides a forum for our top R&D people and group presidents, along with me, to discuss and plan our technology area. This Board meets four times a year and has proved very successful in bringing onto the table the types of concerns I have mentioned.

I think it is a very worthwhile exercise for a company to look back from time to time and examine its history in terms of the things it did right and the things it might have done better. Sometimes, unwritten strategies emerge which, while not planned, clearly were the reasons for success and can be put to even better use for future planning. Our technical strategy was not an overnight planning exercise: It has emerged through the years. The technical area is probably the most difficult of all areas to plan.

Chapter 4
When the Pendulum Swings Toward Applied Research

Roland W. Schmitt
Senior Vice President-Corporate Research and
  Development
General Electric Company

When The Conference Board assigned me the title "When the Pendulum Swings Toward Applied Research," I asked myself ... did the pendulum swing ... and then ... did it swing too little or too far ... and finally ... is it about to swing back the other way, which is what pendulums do?

But, as soon as those questions were asked, I was confronted with a dilemma: These questions have very little to do with the frame of reference of a director of industrial R&D. The variables and parameters implied by those questions do not enter the decisions one has to make about what to do in an industrial laboratory. So, instead of becoming hypnotized by that swinging pendulum—and suffering the fate of unlucky victims in Edgar Allan Poe's famous story, "The Pit and the Pendulum"—I want to escape (as Poe's hero did) by concentrating on the right frame of reference, the right parameters for decisions.

No one will argue very much about the goal of R&D in a corporation: It is, quite simply, to lead and support innovation—product innovation and market innovation for new business development; materials innovation and process innovation for competitive advantage. This R&D occurs at all levels in a corporation and encompasses varying levels of risk and varying degrees of leverage. The most advanced R&D, usually at the corporate level, must devote its energy overwhelmingly to highly leveraged opportunities—the ones that turn entire businesses around, or create entirely new businesses. This advanced R&D should do things like make the first synthetic diamonds, or discover wholly new polymers like LEXAN or NORYL and find cost-effective ways to make them, or put a conventional X-ray business into the new medical

diagnostic technology of Computer-Aided X-ray Tomography—CAT scanning—or invent new light sources, such as Lucalox lamps. To produce such highly leveraged opportunities, one has to do forefront work on a balanced spectrum of programs, and rather than describe this spectrum in terms of basic or applied research, I use the following categories:

- *Today's* focused and targeted projects,
- Work that will produce *tomorrow's* focused and targeted projects,
- Speculative or exploratory work.

These are the variables at the heart of industrial R&D.

Today's Focused and Targeted Projects

Today's highly focused projects are the ones where the target has been identified; where researchers have agreed with the business management about what the product or process is going to be; where the time frame is known; and where the essential challenge is getting leadership product technology out the back door and, with one's business partners, getting the product itself on the market. General Electric's development of the fan-beam CAT scanner in the 1970's is one good example of this type of activity.

Another is our current effort to develop the next major advance in medical diagnostics, the medical use of nuclear magnetic resonance, or NMR. It is a way to take cross-sectional pictures of the head or body without X-rays, and to analyze the body's chemistry without cutting the patient open or sticking any needles into a patient. Along with our partners in GE's Medical Systems

Business Operations, we're converging rapidly on a product. But it will take some very good science and engineering to get there.

It is in this type of work that the pressures are most intense. Those involved encounter unexpected stumbling blocks and can't see how to overcome them in the time allotted. They sometimes feel that razor-sharp pendulum swinging inexorably toward them. They have to make irreversible, critical technical choices. Success depends on a strong, versatile, interdisciplinary cadre of people who are dedicated to the goal, and who are not concerned about whether the work is basic or applied. One needs people who are willing to shift quickly from other programs; to solve the unsolvable; to invent miracles; and to discover the unexpected.

Tomorrow's Focused and Targeted Projects

The second major type of effort is to make sure that there will continue to be opportunities for that kind of targeted effort in the not-too-distant future—namely, when present targeted projects are completed and there are resources to apply to new challenges. This work has much less precisely identified targets, a fuzzy, or maybe even nonexistent, agreement with operations people about what the eventual product or process is going to look like, and a loosely defined time frame.

Sometimes this work originates from the exploratory efforts of researchers. For example, ULTEM, a new high-performance polymer GE introduced last year, began with our discovery of a new class of polymers called polyetherimides. At other times, tomorrow's focused projects grow out of today's focused work, which may open up other windows of opportunity a few years down the road. For example, when some of our researchers were developing ways to put corrosion-resistant coatings on turbine blades, they used a process called vacuum plasma spraying, the spraying of molten droplets onto a surface with an electric arc. In the course of that project, they recognized that the method might permit them to form near-net-shape parts out of superalloys—and get compositions and microstructures not obtainable with other processes.

This project fits into my second category because we have not yet focused it onto specific payoffs, with firm timetables for introducing them. But we are confident that two or three years hence we will have a specific target for hot pursuit. The people needed here are those who can perceive new connections, and who can peer into a hazy arena and spot the potential payoff while others are still focusing their eyes: people with a breadth of understanding of technology, a knowledge of the potential market, and the imagination to put the two together.

Sometimes, that vision has to come from the company's top management—from the general management

level and up. They are the ones with experience and a feel for the market, but without the narrow focus on today's problems, which sometimes afflicts lower management. Sometimes it takes a senior executive to pick the market signal from out of the noise, and to tell us, "There, that's the one to go for."

Exploration

Finally, there is the remaining category of work—exploration. At least a bit of effort should be dedicated to highly speculative ideas. In our laboratory, some examples of this scientific exploration are work in biology, exploring such areas as bacterial genetics and cell growth; computer-assisted quantum mechanical calculations, using fundamental scientific theories to predict the properties of matter; and artificial intelligence.

Those are the categories we use to characterize our effort—today's focused work, opportunities for tomorrow's focused work, and exploration. The balance among them is a dynamic balance that changes with time and shifts back and forth, especially between the first two types. It shifts with the directions taken by GE's businesses, and with the quantity and quality of the new ideas our researchers come up with.

Needed: Balance

Typically, as today's focused projects become better and better identified, the programs need more resources. This can make for tough choices, especially when several emerging targets look promising, but one can not meet the objectives and timing of all of them within the resources available. That means reducing the effort on some projects that are *succeeding*. For example, to build up that NMR effort I mentioned, we had to taper off on a successful program in ultrasonic medical diagnosis; and to strengthen our effort on a new communications method, bandwidth compression, we had to cut back on a successful program on new circuit-board technology. Balancing one's effort among these types of work is probably our greatest management challenge.

There is no simple formula for striking that balance, or for determining the right amount of work in each category. Programs are started and terminated on the basis of the best insights of staff and management as to how to support the present and anticipate the future. Program selection and execution occur in an atmosphere akin to a free marketplace. When the momentum in a particular kind of work is high, the effort will grow, and when demand slackens, or output and results fall below expectations, the effort is reduced or terminated. *After* that process of program definition, selection and execution has taken place on a program-by-program basis, one *can* go back and see what the balance has been between the more conventional categories of research and development.

But even here I do not think the conventional distinction between basic and applied research is useful. For those who do think it is, I suggest the following experiment: Walk down the hallway of a laboratory building, look into one of the individual laboratories, watch the operations that the researcher is carrying out at the bench, and try to judge from that whether the person is doing basic or applied research.

Research versus Development

Let us just talk about *research,* as distinct from *development.* In 1980, about 40 percent of the effort in GE's corporate laboratory was in programs of research; that dropped to 33 percent in 1982, and will be around 25 percent in 1983. This change is *the result* of decisions made in the frame of reference that I have described: today's focused work, opportunities for tomorrow's focused work, and exploration.

And yet this frame of reference for decisions is one that explicitly pays attention to the future as well as the present! It is my contention that research pertains to the present as well as to the future, and that successful research often has short-term payoffs, which contradicts the conventional wisdom that research looks to the future, development to the present; some development must aim for the future as well.

In our case, as we have tried to get a management decision system that relates closely to corporate interests *and* looks at both long and short term, we have found some curious and interesting consequences. Management clearly has become less willing than in the past to support large projects that are almost wholly of a research character. But, concurrently, there is far more willingness to commit to *some* research in a larger cross-section of our programs. Thus, at the time that we are responding to the increasing need of our businesses for strong, highly leveraged technical advances, we are also responding to the need of our development programs for strong research support in relevant, fast-moving areas.

Fundamentally, industrial R&D must face the issues of international competitiveness, efficiency and speed of change—just like other parts of the enterprise. When change is rapid, as it is today, the premium on looking ahead becomes ever greater. And the premium on *today's* successes is greater still. But, the anticipation needed for that future will not come from focusing on a shift from applied to basic research. Nor will success in today's work be helped by timid goals and the swing of a pendulum toward applied work.

What one sees in a successful industrial laboratory are a lot of people who can work in all the various modes I've described: who can come through under pressure when working toward one of those focused targets; who can, when the occasion arises, perceive new targets for tomorrow; and who can, on yet other occasions, take off on an exploration of a new idea, or a campaign of research on a scientific frontier.

In short, one sees a high proportion of scientific and technological entrepreneurs. They are what R&D is all about: not pendulums, but people. Dedicated, creative people shaping a constantly changing, dynamic balance between various types of forefront work.

Good research provides the foundation for each of these types of work. Industrial research and development is not a pendulum swinging between two limits. It is a creative engine, driven by technological entrepreneurs, moving forward into a future that it envisions and shapes.

Chapter 5
Questions and Answers

Question for Dr. Goldman: *Newsweek,* in its article on the Apple LISA computer, described your former Xerox computer science laboratory as a national resource, but indicated that Xerox couldn't or didn't take advantage of the opportunity. Why?

DR. GOLDMAN: An objective evaluation, by which I mean evaluations made by people who are not close enough to the Xerox family to be biased, indeed represented that the laboratory in Palo Alto that I was responsible for creating is a national resource. Somebody at another company recently told me that, in 1975, 60 of the 100 best people in the world in computer science were probably resident at our Palo Alto Research Center. The center was conceived in 1969, and started in 1970. Beginning in 1972, a profusion of new technologies, new ideas, new product opportunities emerged from that laboratory—a profusion that has continued up to the present.

The questioner is quite correct, as was *Newsweek,* because Xerox has hardly made a penny out of the results of that laboratory. In some instances, this was voluntary. When Ethernet was invented, patented and copyrighted, Xerox, as a matter of policy, elected to sell it as what supermarket people might call a "loss leader." That's a euphemism for saying that this type of communications network should be put at the disposal of the community at large because, in the long run, it will help promote the sale of terminals and other devices that attach to the network.

Why did the corporation fail to exploit the great new technologies that emerged out of the center? The answer goes to the nub of what I call the utilization of output. Most large corporations tend not to be entrepreneurial. Getting a new concept or a new product, or even a major modification of an old product, into the pipeline is a major chore when market research and the financial people "nickle and dime" you to the end of the world, when the legal people and the salesmen throw up their own barriers. This is what the small entrepreneurial venture organizations that we see growing up and down the West Coast and Route 128 and some other places today don't have to cope with. And that is why small organizations can accept a new concept. Its investors gamble, but if they are successful, they profit.

Some of the products that came out of the Palo Alto Research Center, had they been in the hands of individual entrepreneurs, would certainly have been successfully launched in the marketplace within a year or two. But for a large enterprise to fold one of these products into its written strategy, to slot the product into a sequence of offerings and national kickoffs and universal rollouts, would be a formidable undertaking. This question really underscores my point that probably the major risk to the corporation is in utilizing output when it transcends present products.

It is probably one of the greatest frustrations of my life that it was Apple that used some of those great new technologies the Palo Alto Center developed, or that little Symbolics near Boston is putting out a laser printer that we invented and had working in the laboratory—and even had in distribution in a couple of spots around the country in 1972. But we delayed for years introduction of this product because of the standards, the service requirements, the sales rollouts, and so forth, that the large company demands before it incorporates a new technology in a product. By the way, it is today a very successful product in the marketplace.

Question for Mr. Krieble: In what ways should the approach of small companies with more limited resources differ from the approach of a large company in their attitudes toward expenditures on research and development?

MR. KRIEBLE: Small companies are generally far more highly focused in regard to the service that they elect to provide, and in the companies or industries with which they choose to do business. Consequently, there is a much smaller chance that any breakthrough in technology outside the narrow scope of the company's mission will help that company. So, at Loctite, we find it not only profitable but absolutely necessary to stay within a pretty small field in order to make our R&D budget work. But take General Electric, with perhaps 150 different businesses within the corporate fold. In a company of that scope, what might be called free-lance research has a fairly high probability of producing something worthwhile.

Question for Dr. Schmitt: GE has a technically qualified chief executive; so does Loctite, obviously. It is alleged here that Xerox did not. Do you think that top management's understanding of technology determines whether R&D has to be treated, as Jack Goldman suggested, as a black box? If so, what can be done to help nontechnical top management understand key technical decisions?

DR. SCHMITT: I guess I'm a very good person to answer that question because our previous chief executive officer was a financial person, and our present one is a technical man. I have to say that they are both strong supporters of technology. The main thing you have to do to get the support of top management is to be successful with technology.

DR. GOLDMAN: May I add something? We had to deal with this problem, since we did not have a technically cognizant top management. As the development and the research on new product lines, particularly in the digital world, went on, there was a larger and larger component of software involved. And we discovered, in the mid-1970's, that top management did not have the slightest grasp of what software was all about. As far as it was concerned, software was just a way of passing instructions to a machine. And when the cost of software started to be comparable to the cost of hardware, top management did not realize that we were dealing with a major new concept in the world's technology. We looked at the future as a future of software factories with "chip labor."

We felt that top management must learn about all this. What I did was bring the key people—the chairman, the president, the executive VP's and the senior VP's, essentially the operating committee of the company—to a three-day software seminar at Palo Alto. We taught them what it was all about; put them at terminals and made them work at the terminals. From that experience, however, they gleaned a certain measure of understanding of what the game of software was about, and why this had now come to represent a significant fraction of the costs of not only R&D, but of product development in general—and even of product maintenance in the field. More generally, I think this educational process for top management is a major chore that R&D managers must face.

Question for Dr. Goldman: If the existing staff is not the best, what do you suggest? A housecleaning? And if

so, how do you combat the effect it has on morale, which you insisted is a sensitive issue?

DR. GOLDMAN: This is not a simple problem, but it is one that anyone recruited from the outside into an organization has encountered. And it is a slow process. I think that abrupt and extensive housecleaning has to be avoided, largely for reasons of morale.

When R&D and the organization in general are growing, the problem is not difficult, because there is a theorem that states that a place can be found for anybody that has achieved some kind of a degree. The place may not necessarily be to the person's liking, and not necessarily in the research enterprise, but there will be a place where an individual can be used. Not infrequently, a mediocre development engineer can become a top-grade technical representative, or a top-grade sales engineer, or systems marketer. We found that we can train people to perform such functions.

But that does not obviate the basic principle that housecleaning, if it is not measured in micro-seconds or even in a semester, but measured in terms of a few years, can be done without necessarily jeopardizing the morale of the organization. One thing is important to anticipate: When top-notch replacements are brought in, they and the people still on the R&D staff will lose patience with each other. The incumbents who are not so good will suddenly realize that they really cannot function like the super-guys, and the super-guys, of course, are not content with the mediocrity of the incumbents. The condition normally reaches equilibrium in a couple of years.

Question for Mr. Krieble: Would you please explain the charter of your Technology Planning Board and the areas on which it focuses, particularly its role with respect to basic research?

MR. KRIEBLE: Our Technology Planning Board is concerned with the future direction of our technology base from which our products are formulated. Issues that have been deeply discussed, for example, are whether or not we should enter the field of structural adhesives, having created, in the huge adhesives industry, our own little market niche of bonding rigid cylindrical fixed parts in machinery. Structural adhesives have quite a different profile of mechanical performance requirements from the typical profile for bonding flat parts, and customers would be of different industry classifications from the customers we now serve.

The board has also discussed the degree to which we should exploit fortuitous discoveries in cures based not only on our historical anaerobic mechanism, but on ultra-violet activation as opposed to free radical activation, or even on daylight frequency initiation (using the ultra-violet light wave frequencies found naturally in daylight to initiate the cure), which again would take us outside of machinery adhesives. The degree to which we should press our technology into consumer applications has been pondered. Should we make the technical expenditures to adapt our products to consumer applications?

The board simply consists of top management meeting with our three laboratory managers on a quarterly basis and looking at the long term, as opposed to following the scheduled progress of new product development.

Question for Dr. Schmitt: Given the enormous number of businesses that General Electric is in, even though you have focused your remarks on some of the concepts or developments which have taken place within the corporate sector, what can you tell us about the successes GE has had in transferring technology developed in the corporate sector effectively into divisional action programs?

DR. SCHMITT: We spend a lot of effort, time and resources on communicating with our operating components, especially those where technology is presumed to have the highest leverage. We have 12,000 visits every year from working line management in engineering and operations. Our people make an enormous number of visits to the operating units. We have a liaison group explicitly charged with understanding the technical gaps and barriers faced by each of our businesses and the opportunities open to them, and with continually acting as lobbyists in our laboratory for those businesses. We have an unending stream of reviews with the individual businesses of the company. The key element in all this is the vast body of information, understanding and data needed to make these linkages fruitful. If that is available, the choices of what to do and what to abandon are not difficult.

Question for the Panel: In your experience, what extra, or special, actions taken by top managements have enhanced the success of R&D programs or laboratories in your companies?

DR. SCHMITT: The situation always changes with each chief executive officer and his unique techniques. Our present chairman is an individual who himself grew up in businesses based on inventions that came out of our laboratory. He likes to tell the story that, when he was in Pittsfield, he used to visit the laboratory there. He would walk through the hallways, telling the scientists what he wanted, finding out what they had, and so on. It was a direct involvement. Today, he is exhorting the senior executives of the company to do likewise.

In his own career, he has made the company a lot of money from inventions and technology that have come out of our laboratories. So he knows what he is talking about, and he knows how to do it. The main problem that I have these days, as we are building new laboratories, adding new wings, and otherwise growing, is reminding the people in my laboratory that he is not rewarding us for things that we have done in the past.

DR. GOLDMAN: I have already mentioned that at Ford the research budget was set for a five-year term, which I think was very salubrious. Another illustration also comes from my days at Ford. About 1960, Henry Ford II decided he wanted a vision of the future world of transportation, a vision that would serve as a guide for all parts of the corporation, including research, in their planning. So he created an interdivisional Transportation Study Task Force. It was an interdisciplinary group of eight or nine people. The members' names are well-known both outside and within the R&D community—people like Don Frey, who was a successor to Bob Charpie at Bell & Howell; people like Arjay Miller, who later became president of Ford, then moved on to the Stanford Business School.

The task force met about once a month. It debated, and commissioned staff studies on, future trends in transportation systems. It produced an annual study for top management and others. Such a study caused me and my associates in research management to focus on energy in the early 1960's. The task force also alerted us to issues in the materials arena, where things should and could be done. All in all, it did have a major impact on the research environment.

Now it may be appropriately asked why the automobile industry, and Ford in particular, suffered the fate it did in the light of dedicated investigation of long-range future trends in transportation. The answer is very simple. Within a short time, six of the original eight people constituting that task force left for one reason or another—retirement, impatience, a better job at Xerox, a desire to go into academic life. They were succeeded by people with gasoline in their veins. They had no patience with what the long-range future would look like. After three or four years, the task force was dissolved.

MR. KRIEBLE: In my experience—I'm not just relying on Loctite but also on some years with two GE laboratories—the most important thing that top management can do to stimulate the R&D function is to treat it like any other function—get it off the pedestal and put it to work. Get rid of the mystique and accept R&D as part of the business team. That implies the most sincere kind of recognition. Then the company will really move innovatively, and it won't have these communication problems or black boxes.

DR. SCHMITT: Bob Krieble almost took the words out of my mouth. I want to support one point Jack Goldman made earlier, and perhaps challenge another. He underscored the importance of excellent people. One of the big dangers in R&D management is that when it is under stress, pressing for results, it will go out and hire the person who can do the immediate job in a hurry. In the long run, that is a destructive trap. What must be done is steadily hiring the best people available. I agree 100 percent with Jack's emphasis on that.

But it is a dangerous fallacy to conclude that outstanding people in the R&D unit should be put on a pedestal, or that they are any kind of elite. By the way, they are not the only people who meet the outside world, contrary to what Jack Goldman said. Marketing people meet the outside world; so do financial people. There are many others who meet the outside world continually.

There is no question about it, a company should be outstanding in R&D. But it also needs people who are outstanding in other fields. For R&D people to consider themselves as some sort of elite is a mistake, for that attitude will interfere with their being part of the management team.

Question for the Panel: In many industries, top managements claim that they are being targeted by foreign competitors or foreign governments. Is there any change of course you would propose for the R&D enterprise or its management in such cases? And do you have any advice for state agencies faced with a base of declining industries to determine which areas of research to support? Keep in mind that many states are now competing for the same high-technology industries.

DR. SCHMITT: States and localities should not emphasize nurturing the same kind of industry. What they ought to do is to concentrate on nurturing the new businesses, or prospective new businesses of whatever kind, which are emerging in their own areas. I don't think there is a place in this country where you cannot find good ideas for starting new businesses. I think the big need in this country today is to establish a climate for entrepreneurship everywhere. The problem is that the climate is not very friendly in many places, and no one seems to know how to make it friendly.

I recently saw for the first time a definition of a high-technology company. It is any business where more than 5 percent of the employees are graduate scientists or engineers. With this definition, it seems to me there are three important roles for high-tech companies to play in the economy. One is to make familiar high-tech products, micro-electronic devices, aircraft engines, and so forth. A second is to apply technology to the smokestack industries. To regain world competitiveness, we have to introduce high technology in these industries as fast as we can from the point of view of productivity and efficiency. The third role is in the services area: I think enormous opportunities exist there, not only for making present services more efficient, but also for opening up entirely new types of services. So there are promising targets for technology in every part of our economy.

MR. KRIEBLE: I agree very much with Roland Schmitt that the critical element is the encouragement of entrepreneurs—entrepreneurs will see to it that the right R&D is developed, and that it is used efficiently in building the economy. Today we are in a situation where there is an abundance of venture capital. There is

growing funding in R&D. But the key guy is the entreprenuer who puts it all together and rebuilds a U.S. economy that has lost its competitiveness, at least in the so-called smokestack industries. I am delighted to see the amount of progress in new start-ups which has been made in the last five years. But we have reached a bottleneck: It is the rate of development of entrepreneurs, not the funding of R&D or funding of venture capital.

DR. GOLDMAN: This gives me an opportunity to ride a favorite hobbyhorse. Silicon Valley and Route 128 are no accident. They are there because of a favorable environment conducive to entrepreneurship and creativity. One aspect is the banking environment in San Francisco Bay Area and in Boston, contrasted with that in the rest of the world. Probably a more important aspect is the attitude of the local universities. When the governor of my state asked me why we are not creating much of a venture-capital economy in Connecticut, I pointed my finger at Yale and said that the university was staying aloof from entrepreneurs, from people who want to start companies. My remark incurred the wrath of President Giamatti, but, notwithstanding that wrath, I think it is a valid comment. Universities have much to contribute. Bill Baker showed that they represent a significant portion of the R&D work going on in the world today. There is a lot of great work going on in universities that will lead to innovation in the ever more important fields of biology, genetic engineering, and CAD/CAM.

But the finger can also be pointed to industries. Large- and medium-sized industries must encourage, as I said earlier, the creation of small enterprises in their backyards. We should see dotting Schenectedy, dotting Westchester County, dotting Detroit, small companies formed by the people who have great ideas, whether they are from universities or from industry, whether or not their enterprises are outgrowths or offshoots of industry. We are beginning to see a bit of this now. Many sizable companies are beginning to invest in smaller entrepreneurial organizations and helping them grow. This trend is a very positive one. For if there is any one type of activity that could override the threat of foreign competition, it is this uniquely American experience, the growth of the small entrepreneur and his encouragement by management, the R&D community and the venture capital world.

Concluding Remarks by Chairman Charpie

If I may be permitted to sum up in one minute what I've learned today, I see a problem, I hear a quotation, and I sense a multipart formula for effective R&D.

We have defined a problem: The changing competitive scene demands new management approaches. Systems engineering techniques (familiar in the military world), software development, access both at home and in the lab to bibliographic updating of what is going on in the world of science, and, ultimately, the incorporation of the emerging techniques of artificial intelligence into our management systems.

The quote? "Challenge is now within management."
The formula?

• Take risks. The first risk is to get high-quality people. It isn't easy, but it is important. The biggest risk is to be prepared to deal vigorously with R&D successes.

• Find ways to relate R&D management in joint planning and evaluation with business management, even for basic research.

• Focused project planning and execution can and do work, but they depend critically on good, broadly based exploratory research. The only research that counts is good research, basic or applied, conducted by technical entrepreneurs of proven ability. Entrepreneurship breeds entrepreneurship.

Part III
Perspectives from Washington

Two officials of the Federal Government contributed their ideas to this conference: Dr. George A. Keyworth, II, Science Advisor to the President and Director, Office of Science and Technology Policy, Executive Office of the President, and Egils Milbergs, Director, Office of Productivity, Technology and Innovation, U.S. Department of Commerce. Dr. Keyworth delivered an address; Mr. Milbergs, chairman of the session on "The Innovative Process: Management's Key Role" (see page 27), made his remarks in introducing that session.

Introductory Remarks

Session Chairman James W. McKee, Jr.
Chairman and Chief Executive Officer
CPC International, Inc.;
Co-chairman and Trustee
The Conference Board, Inc.

At the time of the industrial revolution, the link between science and technology on the one hand and public policy on the other was just beginning to be felt. Had our founding fathers realized the broad impact of the industrial revolution, and the economic and social changes that would follow in its wake, perhaps George Washington or John Adams might have established an office of science and technology policy.

But it was President Eisenhower who established the post of Science Advisor to the President. Dwight Eisenhower was the first of several presidents to feel the need for an expert adviser to help develop policy, to improve current utilization of basic research, to stay abreast or ahead of developing technologies, and, in the long run, to strengthen the competitiveness of U.S. industry in the world market.

In the years between President Eisenhower and President Reagan, science and technology have assumed an even more conspicuous and a much more pervasive role in our lives. A very good case can be made that there are no more critical factors for our survival and well-being than those represented by these two words—science and technology.

Chapter 6
Creating a Climate for Industrial Progress

George A. Keyworth, II
Science Advisor to the President, and
  Director, Office of Science and
  Technology Policy,
Executive Office of the President

The 1960's was a decade of American economic expansion. The 1970's were, as I am sure you have not forgotten, years of rebellion. I am not so foolish as to hazard a prediction for the 1980's, but I do see one trend steadily emerging. Can there be any doubt that in the past few years American assumptions about work and about government have changed? Jobs that had been taken for granted for years, if not for generations, suddenly disappeared. Social programs, many born in an era of seemingly eternal U.S. affluence, began to overwhelm even the resources of the Federal Government, and their rate of growth had to be restrained. Not surprisingly, these and other dislocations have brought understandable public disillusionment and questioning about the causes and about our future.

I have heard some people say that we are at the end of a transition. They claim that the changes were already overdue and appeared suddenly only because we had refused to face reality earlier. Other people cite the beginning of significant new directions in U.S. life. They point to structural unemployment, fierce international industrial competition in technology, and what they see as a shift in the economy from manufacturing to service.

Perhaps both points of view are right. In any case, it is time to recognize that many of the changes are real—that is, they are not some artifact of political ideology that we can legislate away. Our challenge now is to mobilize resources and move ahead. My particular concern as the President's Science Advisor is the Federal Government's appropriate and effective role in research and development, because it is clear that science and technology are important elements in our future.

Well, what should our response to these changes be?

My own belief is that we are seeing a natural, even orderly, evolution in our society. But not everyone shares that view, and my fear is that society will find itself stampeded into reacting hurriedly—and at great expense—to a perceived *crisis* rather than reacting wisely to a real *condition*.

The distinction between a crisis and a condition is not always obvious. A recent article in *Forbes* magazine offered an interesting perspective on one of these supposed U.S. crises, the much-discussed shift from a goods-producing economy to a service economy. It was interesting for two reasons. First, the author claimed that we are engaged in a new debate about an old situation, because the United States has been increasingly a service economy for the past 40 years. He then went on to argue that thinking about production and service as fundamentally separate industries misleads us as we attempt to understand where our economy is heading.

His thoughts struck a responsive chord, because I can see a parallel to current perceptions about the impact of "high technology" on our industry. High technology is not much more than a fancy term to describe the application of new knowledge to whatever we do. Those people who think of high technology only in terms of microelectronics and genetic engineering miss an essential point: that perhaps the more important impact—more important even than the development of brand new industries—may be in how our traditional industries and services can be steadily improved by better technology.

The *Forbes* writer offered the opinion that even though we would all agree that a Boeing 747 is a very tangible manufactured product, we could as well think of it as the means to provide a pure service—transportation.

Similarly, I would observe that even though we all agree that a Chevrolet is not an exotic, high-technology product, it is nonetheless the product itself of increasingly high-technology manufacturing techniques. I invite those people who think they can draw a firm line between high tech and low tech, or, worse, who think that in our society government could direct the development of specific high-technology industries, to take another look at how modern commerce evolves.

Finally, as an introduction to my discussion of how the Federal Government is helping the U.S. industrial capacity to grow, I can't resist quoting a wise passage from that same article. The author, James Cook, says:

"In the end, the wealth-producing forces of any economy are its *immaterial resources*—not oil or gas, copper or iron ore, but rather the intellectual and organizational skills that are the very core of the services."[1]

I want to review those immaterial resources, and how government is making an extraordinary commitment to sustaining them.

This commitment is clearly seen in the President's request for large increases of federal funds to support basic research in the coming fiscal year. This focus on science is an end result of a year-long effort in the White House to identify how the Federal Government could assure the strengthening of the nation's economy, and particularly the health of our industries. Our goal is self-sustaining long-term growth—growth that does not require constant federal intervention or subsidization of the marketplace. We are determined to strengthen our free-enterprise system so U.S. industry can compete aggressively in the international marketplace—and so that it can create the jobs and profits that we expect from a healthy economic system.

International competition—especially in high-technology industries and in those industries that depend on technology—has been an obvious focus of our attention. The situation today is unsettling, though we may have overreacted to recent business downturns. Sometimes we have failed to distinguish between industrial attenuation due to general economic sluggishness, and loss of markets due to foreign competition. In fact, most U.S. industry is very strong and highly productive, and we will see reassuring evidence of that as economic demand picks up this year.

Still, we would be foolish to ignore the trends. Foreign industries *are* becoming better in those very high-technology fields we look to for our own prosperity. But

the problems for real concern are not what is going to happen in the next year or so, but where U.S. industry may be a decade down the road.

I want to insert a strong caution here against a rising undercurrent of protectionism in this country. We can not solve trade problems by isolating domestic industries from the international marketplace. We would seriously damage long-term U.S. productivity if we were to shrink from competition, as some people are advocating in various protectionist proposals. As the President has pointed out, protectionism eliminates as many American jobs in one sector as it purports to save in another. Moreover, protectionism virtually ensures a continuing decline in competitiveness for a protected industry. That approach mortgages the future and prices those industries out of international markets—hardly a far-sighted policy in today's world.

This issue of trade policy has been heavily debated in the White House, where the broad issues of both near-term and long-term industrial health have occupied a great deal of the President's time in the past year. At his insistence, we have been weighing an astonishing variety of issues and problems that bear on our industrial competitiveness. As might be expected, in addition to trade, these include capital formation, antitrust, patent revisions, regulatory relief, and tax policy. The number of ways suggested to approach industrial problems confirms both their complexity and their importance.

What Is Needed

One conclusion that emerged time and time again was that we have to give high priority to producing more skilled scientific and technical personnel. Our current rate of training, though adequate in most fields during the recession, would fall critically short of our needs as the economy picks up steam. One of our major concerns is that shortages of scientists and engineers could actually be a brake on economic expansion because so much of the fastest growth will be in technology-intensive fields. And in today's highly competitive world, industrial opportunities will pass us by if we have to scurry to train new talent.

Another conclusion, not surprising, was that we have to ensure that we continue to generate new knowledge in those areas with the most likely impact on new technology and industrial and defense needs. Those two circumstances led fairly directly to the decision to emphasize funding for physical sciences and engineering. Research done in universities also supports and trains graduate students under what are surely the most stimulating intellectual conditions anywhere. But few people realize how many graduate students are supported by that mechanism. Federally sponsored research projects in universities support more than 30,000 graduate students each year.

[1]James Cook, "You Mean We've Been Speaking Prose All These Years?" *Forbes,* April 11, 1983.

This mechanism will go a long way toward increasing the supply of technical personnel. But we also know that some pressing personnel problems *won't* be adequately addressed by these increases in research support. For that reason, we have proposed several additional ways to address what we believe is another critical problem—the inadequate supply of new junior engineering and science faculty in universities, and the shortage of qualified secondary school science and math teachers.

These programs have already been described in some detail on other occasions. I would just say that we expect the new Presidential Young Investigator Awards to attract recent Ph.Ds to university jobs—people who might not otherwise pursue teaching careers. And several other programs would improve the supply of qualified science and math teachers in secondary schools. These are high-leverage programs that concentrate resources strictly where they are most needed, on good faculty. We anticipate substantial long-term benefits.

A third element of our concern about industry's health was how to address a well-known paradox: We have the dominant and best basic research capability in the world, but some other countries do a better job than we do of using new knowledge for industrial advances. In light of the size of the Federal Government's investment—$15 billion of the taxpayers' money for civilian R&D next year, of which $6 billion is for basic research—this is a deeply troubling situation. In today's budget climate, activity of that magnitude has to be scrutinized for how well it meshes with national priorities.

We have made significant progress in redirecting R&D in the past two years, although there is more still to be done. Just think for a moment about our most pressing national needs; then consider that there are still institutions claiming a large portion of those federal R&D resources that do not contribute significantly to training scientific personnel; do not contribute significantly to improving industrial productivity; and do not contribute significantly to improving national defense. And some of these institutions, it must be added, are not particularly at the forefront of scientific research either. What, then, are they doing that's so important?

I am afraid many of my colleagues in the world of science have gotten too comfortable with the notion that federal support for R&D is an entitlement, that it is going to come off the top of the budget independent of economic pressures or national priorities. Well, it's not. We have been trying over the past two years to impress on the research community that it has an important role to play in this country's future. But it *has* to come to grips with the realities of the 1980's.

One of my chores in recent months has been to disabuse them of any idea that the increase in support for academic research is a reward for all the supposed fine things the basic research community has been doing. It is *not* a reward: It is a *challenge* to the universities to

assume a greater role in helping us regain our momentum in world technological leadership.

How can we do a better job of taking advantage of that capability? Naturally, the increases in support for basic research are important, but bear in mind that our real concern is for quality of research, not quantity. Larger numbers of projects, or even larger numbers of scientists and engineers, do not automatically produce leadership.

For that reason, our first priority now is to permit the *best* research to be more fully supported so that it's influence can be extended in the field. This is the time to do a job with the *best* tools we have, not a time to dissipate our resources by parceling them out in response to popular demand—and, believe me, there is no lack of demand.

Isolation a Problem

Earlier I explained how the concern for strengthening American industrial competitiveness led to these emphases on basic research and training. There is another outcome. U.S. technological progress suffers—and sometimes suffers badly—from the artificial barriers between industry and the bulk of the basic research establishment. Most academic and federal scientists still function in virtual isolation from the expertise of industry. They derive little benefit from the experience and guidance of the marketplace. One can make a convincing case that this separation is a root cause of our sluggishness, compared with some of our more energetic competitors, in turning research into products.

I am always puzzled that so much of the academic research community has failed to notice how successful and mutually beneficial those industrial interactions are. At least a few universities have demonstrated that academic research can both achieve the highest levels of quality and also be linked to the industrial world for great economic and intellectual benefit. Places like MIT and Stanford should be beacons for the community. The proliferation of new, technically oriented industries along Route 128 outside of Boston is no coincidence, nor is the prosperity of Silicon Valley. Both were stimulated by alert academic communities, and both in turn have returned stimulation to the universities.

Universities are not alone in this isolation. We are looking for innovative responses from *other* research institutions, too, such as the federal laboratories. Many of those labs, which were established decades ago to deal with highly specific national problems, are no longer focusing on problems of first-line importance. But they are still valuable resources—good people, good facilities—and we intend to put them to better use.

I admit that's easier to say than to do—and it takes patience, much like steering an ocean liner. We moved the rudder two years ago, and we're finally beginning to sense a change of course. One example of what I think is an exciting prospect for a new level of interaction between academic, federal and industrial scientists is The Center for Advanced Materials Research being established at Lawrence Berkeley Laboratory.

There are two things to realize about the LBL project. One is that the United States is in a position to consolidate and expand its leadership in materials science. And it is obvious that better materials will be critical to a host of future industrial technologies. This Center will bring outstanding talent to bear on this area of research. But even more important, in the long run, is what LBL learns and teaches the rest of us about how academic, federal and industrial scientists and engineers can collaborate on research of mutual interest.

LBL is a prototype—or maybe test bed would be a more accurate description—for the kind of mixing of different research viewpoints that will eventually focus research better, and will certainly speed up the transfer of new knowledge to the marketplace. I think we ought to applaud LBL's willingness to venture into this uncharted territory, and we ought to do whatever we can to help the materials science program succeed.

We want to be bolder still in trying out new ways for industry to work more closely with the basic research community. The example of Lawrence Berkeley Laboratory; the shared funding of science education programs; the expansion of industrial research at places like the National Synchrotron Light Source at Brookhaven National Laboratory; our increasing determination that the national labs should incorporate greater private-sector perspectives in their management—all these are attempts to use our massive resources better.

Let me be quite frank: In the kinds of programs I am describing, the money contributed by industry is not the real issue. What we are counting on are the payoffs from new perspectives, from imparting a better sense of the reality and stimulation of the marketplace to a basic research community that has become increasingly isolated over the decades. We are still in the early stages of this process; many of these efforts are exploratory. But we really need to stimulate some fresh thinking. One thing is certain: The creativity and innovations are not likely to come from Washington. I freely admit that I can't—and I won't—tell a place like Oak Ridge National Lab, or Caltech, or General Motors how to develop cooperative programs, or how to link public- and private-sector interests. At best, the Federal Government can create a *climate* to encourage those things—and it can make a commitment to *maintaining* that climate.

Two Caveats

I want to comment briefly on a distinction that is increasingly blurred these days—the difference between policies and programs. The political rhetoric is heating up, and we're hearing a lot of talk about the need for a grandiose U.S. "industrial policy." Actually, I think I have just described part of a pretty sensible policy: the Administration's approach to strengthening the science and technology base for industrial growth in the future. But it turns out that most of these calls for an industrial policy are, in reality, calls for an industrial program. Not surprisingly, the Administration parts company there from those who think the government is better suited than industry to sniff out and develop tomorrow's technology.

There are also those who believe that if we just spend enough on science and technology, then U.S. industry will make technological leaps. But we have already tried that. In the 1970's, the Federal Government spent enormous amounts of money on science. But that science was largely unconnected to the reality of the marketplace, and it was precisely during those same years that we began to lose the overwhelming technological lead we had enjoyed for decades. Yet today we hear renewed assertions that the solution to technological competition is a guaranteed funding level for R&D, some fixed percentage of the GNP. Aside from what I predict would be the failure of that mechanism to hold up in the brutal give and take of budgetmaking, I have already indicated my own distaste for trying to turn R&D into an entitlement.

Why? Because that attitude is deadly to good science. The first entitlement begets more. Pretty soon, we have individual disciplines demanding their guaranteed share of the pie; then regional demands for portions. Next we would be divvying up portions among universities, four-year colleges, and two-year colleges. All too soon the *only* criterion that ought to count—excellence—would be lost in the noise of formula grants, geographic distribution, and set-asides. We can't let that happen in science, and we can't let that happen in commerce.

* * *

Following his remarks Dr. Keyworth responded to questions on several topics.

Delineating the proper federal role. This is necessarily judgmental. One conclusion we reached in the course of many Cabinet councils and discussions is that ensuring that there will be sufficient talent for tomorrow is a federal trust. But we have realized that much of the federal involvement in development and demonstration activities—characterized, for example, by the emphasis, in the last ten years, on federal support of synthetic fuels development—is not in the nation's best interests in the long-run. It is neither conducive to assuring that the right technology is pursued at the right time, nor is it a competitive use of scarce federal funds.

It is not a question of whether the Federal Govenment could spend a dollar wisely, or usefully, for the nation's betterment; it is a question of priorities. There are very few fields into which the Federal Government should venture, the nuclear arena being one.

Revising antitrust laws to encourage cooperative industry-sponsored R&D ventures. I think I can speak without attempting to represent the entire Administration's views, including the Department of Justice's. To me, as a nuclear physicist, it is a very simplistic issue. I cannot understand why laws that were designed to ensure free competition in a domestic market when the international marketplace was remote must be allowed to constrain our ability to compete against forces like Japanese targeting. Not that this is immoral. There are few countermechanisms available to us to preserve our free-enterprise environment. It would seem to me that cooperative R&D ventures in many areas would be healthy in enhancing our ability to compete.

A U.S. MITI? Have we thought about transferring the Department of Commerce into a Japanese MITI (Ministry of International Trade and Industry)? Well, first of all, in this Administration we have to think about it very very quietly. I think that the MITI technique is justifiable when a nation is trying to pull itself out of the trough of a devastating world war, trying to modernize itself. I do not think that the majority of Americans would like to see us embrace a MITI concept. Our past efforts in trying to involve government directly in determining our marketplace prospects and directions for the future have not been consonant with traditional U.S. principles. Nor do I believe an American-style MITI would be effective.

But the Department of Commerce could have a stronger impact than it does on our trade position, as well as on our productivity and innovativeness. It is now trying to do so. It is looking deeply into how it might create a better climate for the forces of international competition to function.[2]

I believe that the United States can respond to MITI

[2]See the remarks of Egils Milbergs on pages 27-28.

and its targeting very, very effectively. I think we are doing so. In the last two years, I have seen an enormous amount of vision creep into the leadership of American industries. I think as a nation we are responding to competitive challenges. Unfortunately, a long time passed before we really saw how serious those challenges were.

Technology transfer policy. There are no problems more complex than the issue of technology transfer. No two people see it identically. I think the two bounds to the problem are, first, we should never threaten our academic institutions, our basic research establishment, by believing that knowledge, by itself, is threatening when transferred.

Second, we must be very very careful about certain critical technologies (the application of science, not the science itself): for instance, anti-submarine technology, anti-stealth technology, stealth technology itself, and, of course, the key technologies that sustain America's leadership in micro-processors—the kinds of things we do not want to the Soviet Union to obtain. Russia's intelligence and information-gathering means have been unbelievably effective. There is virtually a one-to-one comparison between every single step forward that has been taken in Soviet military technology in the last 20 years and a preceding step taken here. We exposed the B-1 bomber; they delivered a Rampee Bomber.

But let us not incite paranoia in ourselves. There are people who are absolutely paranoid on the subject of technology transfer. Instead of worrying so much about technology transfer from here to a European ally, or wherever, we should stimulate the kind of transfer I tried to address in my talk, from the laboratory to the marketplace.

I assure you there are different positions within *any* Administration about technology transfer. That is healthy, and I think the issue will be resolved sensibly. But I cannot tell you that we have resolved it. It is still an ongoing issue that is terribly complicated by an entrenched bureaucracy.

Chapter 7
The Federal Government's Role and Its Programs

Egils Milbergs
Director, Office of Productivity, Technology and
  Innovation
U.S. Department of Commerce

The Office of Productivity, Technology and Innovation has as its major responsibility the exercise of policy and program direction to stimulate U.S. productivity growth and technological competitiveness. As a nation, we are clearly pinning our hopes on new technology as a means of achieving future economic growth, international competitiveness, the creation of jobs, and improving product quality and productivity. And we are witnessing an explosion of new technology in such areas as information transfer and new materials, factory and office automation, biotechnology, and medicine, to mention just a few.

It is clear that the nation is in the midst of a major transition marked by continuous restructuring of the economy. It is important to realize that while general economic conditions are now improving and will improve over the next few months and, we hope, the next few years, we will also need to be concerned with the direction and magnitude of this restructuring, so that its consequence will be to make us again a world-class competitor.

The impact of these new technologies will be significant, particularly on the private sector. They will make capital investments obsolete long before their useful lives can be amortized. They will also render obsolete more rapidly technical and managerial skills. They will shorten product and industry life cycles. They will make it possible for one industry to invade or challenge another industry. Electronic funds transfer, for example, will permit retailers like Sears Roebuck to become competitive with the banking industry. Cable television may become very competitive with the printing business. Finally, new technologies will call into question—indeed, are already doing so—such public policies as antitrust laws and such regulatory structures as in the communications sector.

Government policymakers and private management will also need to respond to the targeting strategies aimed at capturing market share in emerging technologically intensive markets. These strategies, pioneered by Japan and now copied by others, have already had a devastating impact on many sectors of our economy, old and new, and in the 1980's they will focus on personal computers, 256-K and million-bit memory chips, robotics, satellite communications, engineering plastics, ceramics and biotechnology. The net effect of this technological explosion and international competition will be a period of rapid and continuous change, entailing a continual reevaluation of public policy and management practices.

Let me say a few words to reinforce George Keyworth's remarks about the role of government. We see our role as creating a climate, a framework, an atmosphere for private-sector initiative in response to these challenges. Innovation is a long, multi-step process beginning with an idea, followed by evaluating its technical and commercial feasibility, setting up pilot programs, and commercializing its product or service. It is up to the government to (1) eliminate externally imposed barriers to this process; (2) provide catalytic support in the way of information, education and technical assistance; (3) design incentives to facilitate the innovative process; and (4) encourage new institutional relationships among industry, universities and the public sector. We do not believe it is the government's role to dictate, to direct, to select winners and losers, or to guarantee success. All that is the job of the private sector.

How the Government Is Fulfilling Its Role

A new Department of Commerce program is encouraging the use of R&D limited partnerships to raise money for R&D and for the subsequent commercialization of new products and processes. The use of such a partnership is an alternative to in-house funding or joint R&D arrangements.[1]

Better education at all levels is vital to future technological growth, and so we have been working with the National Science Foundation to spend $35 million to recognize superior teaching and to improve secondary teaching of science and math. There will also be a matching fund program with the private sector to provide awards to 200 new Ph.D.'s in technical disciplines, and to aid universities in faculty retention. Still being debated in Congress is an Administration proposal to provide block-grant money to aid states in bettering their math and science teaching.

On February 18, the President directed the federal agencies to allow nearly all federal R&D contractors the right to own federally funded innovations. This broadens a previous policy of permitting private ownership only by small businesses and nonprofit organizations, such as universities.

We are also trying to increase private-sector commercialization of technology developed in federal laboratories. We have established a center for the utilization of federal technology which provides ways and means to help U.S. firms locate government technology of potential commercial interest. We have revitalized a program that actively promotes the licensing of government-owned inventions with significant commercial potential.

The Treasury Department, the Department of Commerce, the Council of Economic Advisors, and the Office of Management and Budget are evaluating the effectiveness of tax policy pertaining to R&D. A specific issue is the 25-percent incremental tax credit; we shall be assessing options for making the credit permanent, as well as the pros and cons of broadening its definition of R&D to include the nonmanufacturing sector of the economy, and how the credit might be able to benefit start-up ventures more appropriately.

The Administration will formally propose to Congress a legislative package that would cut back on antitrust penalties for joint research arrangements, deal with the treble-damage issue, and remove joint research arrangements from the *incubus* or *succubus* of per se violations. We shall be expanding protection for patents, copyrights and trademarks. Later this year, a White House conference on productivity will be held to generate more ideas about improving productivity and technological competitiveness. And the President will be announcing a commission on industrial competitiveness in the near future.

All these actions are aimed at helping the private sector manage its R&D programs and its technological assets. Our job, as I said, is to remove barriers, to create an encouraging environment, and to provide appropriate incentives.

[1]See the Department of Commerce brochure, *Large Scale R&D Partnerships*. Available from the Assistant Secretary for Productivity, Technology and Innovation, Room 4824, 14th and Constitution Avenue N.W., Washington, D.C., 20230, or any Department of Commerce Field Office.

Part IV
Organizing For R&D
Chairman: Robert E. Wilson
Senior Vice President and Director
Heidrick and Struggles

Chapter 8
The Centralized Research Organization

Leo J. Thomas
Senior Vice President and Director of the
   Kodak Research Laboratories
Eastman Kodak Company

In discussing the pros and cons of centralized research, I will concentrate on three observations drawn from my perspective as director of the Kodak Research Laboratories.

The first observation is that organizational structure alone—either centralized or decentralized—does not make an effective laboratory. The key to effective research is ultimately the people you have to work with. This is not a new insight. Nearly 50 years ago, the first director of research at Kodak, Dr. C.E. Kenneth Mees, addressing the issue of research organization at a meeting of the National Research Council, said: "Different laboratories seem to have very different methods of working, and as far as I can see, there is no relation between the methods used and the results achieved, from which I conclude that the type of organization doesn't matter very much and what does matter is the caliber of men who form the organization."

My second observation is that research organizations are really a function of history: Over a period of time, organizations evolve to serve the needs, goals and objectives of the business. As such, it is difficult to argue that a centralized structure, such as the one we have at Kodak, is intrinsically better than a decentralized organization. It might be better for Kodak, as we shall see, but not as appropriate for Johnson & Johnson, or any other large and complex corporation.

And third—but perhaps most important—whatever organizational structure is in place, it must function to minimize mismatches with other company functions. Let us assume that the goals of research are compatible with the goals of general management: Then the organizational structure of the laboratory must have an effective way of relating to the rest of the company.

Evolution

The early history of Eastman Kodak Company is the story of the evolving nature of a set of core technologies, a principal one being silver halide emulsion technology. The business was founded on this basic technology, and growth resulted when research applied the technology across a range of products. For example, variations on the black-and-white film technology for picture taking were soon serving medical diagnostics and business applications. Growth then became a matter of taking an established technological base and adding to it through innovation.

This factor itself made centralized research practical for Kodak. But just as important was the way the manufacturing organization was evolving. It, too, would be highly centralized. There was a key reason: The same machine could be used to manufacture different kinds of film, whether black-and-white camera films, X-ray films, or microfilm. The principle of applying thin layers of emulsion at high speed fit all film manufacturing situations. Thus, a highly integrated, functional manufacturing organization grew naturally for Kodak. Apparatus manufacturing is, of course, also a major activity at Kodak. And although it is distinct from film manufacture, the two are highly integrated because of the unique traditional linkage of film and cameras in Kodak's business.

If our portfolio of products had been highly unrelated, requiring very different types of facilities, perhaps in widely separated geographic locations, the situation would have been very different. Not only would manufacturing have been decentralized, it is likely that the research to support manufacturing and product development would have been decentralized as well.

In line with the historical pattern, then, the centralized research function at Kodak grew naturally. Movement into new product areas based on silver halide was a matter of building on established technology. The technical base might encompass 80 percent of the scope required to develop a new product. New areas of technical work would be added to make up the final 20 percent required to arrive at a marketable product.

Research and development of complex products requires close cooperation among a variety of disciplines within our laboratories. The introduction several years ago of the Kodak Ektachem blood analyzer is one example of the benefits we derive from the centralized laboratory, and how we build new products from an established technological base. The Ektachem blood analyzer is a relatively new product in a segment of the health-care market we had not served before. It uses dry chemistry and complex instrumentation for precise blood testing. And it is a product that reflects our traditional strength in chemical research, in coating technology, in colorimetrics, and in instrumentation. This expertise alone, however, was not enough to carry us successfully into a new market. So we added another discipline to our research capability: biotechnology. And our centralized organization brought together all of these disciplines—chemists, physicists, film formulation experts, and biotechnologists—in an environment that provided the mix of expertise and know-how required to produce a new product breakthrough.

Of course, a major challenge in the management of centralized research is to keep innovation flowing, and to make sure the organizational structure encourages rather than hinders this innovation. When Dr. Mees opened the Kodak Research Laboratory in 1912, there were only 20 scientists working with him. This situation lent itself to frequent and ongoing communication. He had a close relationship with Eastman, and they had many opportunities to exchange ideas on the functions of industrial research. It is an interesting historical footnote that the Research Laboratory was the first Kodak organization to have a formal budget. And it was Mees who asked for one, rather than Eastman forcing it upon him. In fact, Eastman's reaction to the request was one of surprise. "Why do you want a budget?" he asked. "You always get what you ask for." But Mees replied that a budget would assure a continuity of funds not only during good times, but during those times when things might not be doing so well.

Today, approximately 8,000 scientists are involved in Kodak research and development worldwide. Although the central thrust of our research is in Rochester, there are also laboratories in England, France and Australia. These overseas labs have provided us with payoffs that Rochester alone could not have delivered—if for no other reason than that they have sometimes taken a different approach to a problem. These laboratories represent a decentralized element within an overall centralized structure. There is another laboratory in Tennessee: It is a part of the Eastman Chemicals Division and serves our chemicals, plastics and fibers business.

Present Organization

Obviously, Mees' somewhat "formless" approach to research would not be practical today for an organization with a $700 million budget, serving a worldwide business with sales of nearly $11 billion. How, then, are we organized today?

While marketing units are structured to reflect the use of finished products such as consumer items, business systems, medical products, and so on, research is organized principally by technical areas. This is necessary to serve a diverse produce line based on overlapping technologies. These areas include color photography, electronics, and nonsilver halide research. Each of these areas may be interdisciplinary. Most encompass activities from basic research through product development, and most are applied to the problems of more than one business. Traditional color imaging, for example, is applied to markets in photofinishing, consumer photography, and motion-picture products. On the other hand, coating technology covers virtually all product areas. Each research division has a director who is responsible for a number of laboratories.

A major disadvantage of a centralized structure is its tendency to stifle the flow of innovative ideas from the laboratories. One way we try to get around this problem is through our Scientific and Technical Advisory Committee. It is made up of senior research associates who represent each of the laboratories. They are among our most experienced and knowledgeable scientists and they provide access to lab management. (Editors' note: For more information on this committee, see Chapter 12, page 47.)

We see a number of plus factors in centralized R&D that outweigh the minuses. One is that we can achieve economies of scale when it comes to capital investment in facilities. We have been able to consolidate our most expensive analytical and testing equipment in two divisions, which serve the needs of all others. Film-coating technology, for example, is applied in traditional color photography, instant photography, and emulsion research. Some sophisticated coating machines cost millions of dollars, so it would be impractical and inefficient to supply each division with all its own machines. The same is true for expensive analytical equipment. Instruments for photon spectroscopy or liquid chromatography can range from several thousand dollars to approximately one-half million dollars.

Another advantage of centralized research is that there

are no geographical boundaries to overcome. Centralized organization provides the atmosphere for interaction among specialties, disciplines and technical people who seek to apply the accumulated weight of expertise to a project. This interaction can be formal or informal. Informally, it may be as routine as a chemist and a physicist meeting in the hallway to discuss an idea. Or on a more organized basis, it can be encouraged through the formation of interdisciplinary or interdivisional teams of scientists.

The ability to marshal large numbers of people and resources for major projects is a third advantage of the centralized laboratory. This was a definite advantage during the development of the disc photography system, which was introduced last year. The development of disc-system technology involved the entire Kodak organization. It required an R&D interface with every major unit of the company, from film and camera manufacturing to marketing. We not only had to devise new electronics and optics technology to make the camera easy to use and capable of quality results, we had to build a whole new film.

We were able to assemble a multidisciplinary task force for traditional color photography. The task force's goal was to carry forward the research required for a new photographic system. There was a high level of interaction among all of these researchers. The group started small, but grew as the project moved toward completion. It remained unstructured in the hierarchial sense, and members operated as coequals. To maintain continuity within the group, laboratory heads had to resist temptations to pull members out for other, short-term projects or for "firefighting." Our centralized organization helped to foster this cooperation in the sense that laboratory managers were part of the planning process that established the task-force mechanism. They knew the priorities and were in agreement with them.

People Count

It should be emphasized that the success of the task force was not ultimately based on the type of organization set up to carry out the research. The quality of the people involved was far more important than the structure. If the structure deserves any credit, it is that it provided the flexibility to let people pursue the course fully. To a real degree, an organizational structure should be viewed as neutral or negative. An organizational structure can do one of two things: (1) It can let people perform at the level they are capable of achieving, or (2) it can impede performance. In other words, you can't improve research quality by simply organizing better. Suppose a group of people are capable of performing at a level arbitrarily set at 100. There is nothing you can do organizationally that will make them perform at 110. But there certainly are things that you can do that will make them perform at 90 or 80, or even 10.

People, then, are the vital raw material of successful R&D. The purpose of the organization is to get the most out of them, whether that organization is centralized or decentralized. And that is the responsibility of laboratory management. An organization, over a period of time, will seldom outperform its management. Poor management makes it very difficult to get good results out of good people. This is, of course, tied to my observation that any research organization must be functionally compatible with the other elements of the corporation. It must be organized so that management is comfortable with dealing with it—and sees it as a useful tool for profitability.

To a large extent, doing research is somewhat akin to "pushing on a rope." If research is going to have any impact, results must flow smoothly into the other functions of the company. If they do not, no matter what the quality of research, it will be ineffective. In a number of U.S. companies, during the last 20 years, we have seen a lack of research payoff because of a mismatch between the research technical capability—which may have been outstanding—and the company's business goals.

Linkages and Planning

One way to overcome this problem is to link research closely with all elements of the corporation: manufacturing, marketing and, most important, top management. This linkage provides the communications channels required for mutual understanding of corporate and research objectives. A key function of Kodak research is to support existing business by extending the reach of in-place technology. By being organized to enhance problem solving on the manufacturing floor and to provide evolutionary product improvements, research ensures its role in shaping the company's day-to-day profitability picture. It also ensures the attention of management.

The other critical function of Kodak research is to support the future growth of the company. This means discovering and developing the new technology to be applied in tomorrow's products. To assure that the search for tomorrow's technology is consistent with where management wants to go, there is strong linkage to top management through the strategic-planning mechanisms. R&D's involvement in this process is essential if innovation is to be directed toward serving market needs and if research is going to have any influence on the direction the company might take in the future.

At Kodak, research involvement cuts across the range of planning functions from new-but-undefined product opportunities to implementation of current product strategies. We have our own strategic-planning process in the labs, and it links with similar activities in the major operating divisions of the company. We prepare our plan by technical areas, going through the process of defining the technology, assessing boundaries, and discussing businesses on which it can have an impact. We try to assess how well we are doing in the technology relative to others, evaluating strengths and weaknesses against competing technologies. We spell out product or process objectives over a ten-year period, and we describe how we plan to get where we want to go.

Copies of these plans are sent to top management and to appropriate people in finance, marketing, manufacturing and corporate planning. We then follow up with presentations and discussions that include all groups that ought to influence, or be influenced by, these plans. There is an opportunity to challenge these plans and to suggest other objectives. I have oversimplified this communication process: It is highly iterative at several levels, but it provides an excellent vehicle for communication.

In carrying out the corporate plans, research people serve on steering committees and other coordinating groups along with people from the other corporate functions. These contacts are a major communication vehicle for us. The communication receives a lot of emphasis—and it should. As I said before, we have a functional organization, and no function can carry a project all the way from start to finish. Through this planning process, R&D is coupled into the basic decisions of the company. It gives R&D management a mechanism through which it can guide research to lead the company where it wants to go.

The matter of functional research is a key point I'd like to make. As I said at the outset, structure can be overemphasized. No matter how people are organized, they can turn out good research. But that research must serve a function—to advance the growth of the business. The structure should serve this end. The historical thrust of Eastman Kodak Company's business led to a centralized organizational structure. It allows us to achieve economies of scale and the interdisciplinary cross-fertilization required for a diverse product line based on overlapping technologies. And it allows us to marshal the resources and people necessary to carry out the major programs on which the company's future is based.

With ample funding, a pragmatic focus, and sufficient freedom and flexibility, we believe it is possible to use our centralized R&D organization to allow our people to produce what we believe is high-quality research.

Chapter 9
Decentralized R&D Organization

Robert A. Fuller
Corporate Vice President-Science and Technology
Johnson & Johnson

The type of research and development organization suitable for a particular corporation depends on many factors, such as its history, its structure, what I would call its psyche (which its history has a lot to do with), its geographical spread, the degree of technical diversity involved, its general business strategy, (particularly with respect to the emphasis placed on technology), the businesses it is in or it wants to be in, and its relative size and diversification. The mode of organization will perhaps have to change if significant changes are made in one or more of these factors. However, whether the present organization is actually working or not is obviously much more important than any theoretical arguments as to which system might better serve a company's needs. As Jack Thomas suggested, although Kodak and Johnson & Johnson have very different systems, each has served its company well.

There are two somewhat conflicting points of view in approaching the organization of research and development. One is concerned with the organization of the R&D operation per se, and the other with the organization of R&D activity as part of the total enterprise. For a large company with several locations, as we have, and many product lines, the fundamental problem is reduced to one of centralization versus decentralization. The consideration of the organization of R&D activity, however, should not be viewed in terms of either absolute centralization or absolute decentralization, but rather as a spectrum stretching from one to the other. Lowell Steele, in his book *Innovation in Big Business,* has described several different points on this spectrum.[1] One extreme is Bell Labs, which performed all of the technical work on research and advanced

development and design and systems engineering for the equipment used in the AT&T subsidiaries. Moving away from the highly centralized paradigm, he examines different degrees of decentralization involving various combinations of centralized and decentralized activities, sometimes involving geographical separation, sometimes not, and with varying degrees of coupling between a central lab and decentralized affiliates. At the other end of that spectrum are companies in which all of the R&D work is carried out on a decentralized basis, where each individual unit (a division or a company) is self-sufficient in R&D. There are examples of such organizations both with and without a corporate staff function to assist in coordination and to provide an overview for the senior corporate management. Johnson & Johnson is situated at this end of the spectrum—decentralized R&D, with only very recent formation of a corporate staff function.

The existence of differing successful organizational schemes illustrates that there is not a right and wrong organizational arrangement for research and development. Each system has advantages and disadvantages, or perhaps it is better to say strengths and weaknesses, because there are ways to overcome most of the potential disadvantages. The essential thing, of course, is to establish and maintain the proper environment for maximum creativity and productivity in the R&D function and successful innovation in the corporation. As in all areas of management, the most important ingredient, as others have said, is competent people, both in the R&D operation itself and in the management to whom the R&D function reports.

Potential Advantages of Decentralized R&D

Let us look at some of the potential advantages of decentralized R&D. Individual business units (for us that means approximately 150 companies which are given a

---

[1]Lowell W. Steele, *Innovation in Big Business.* New York: Elsevier, 1975, pp. 118-120.

mission and the necessary freedom of action to carry it out) do not confront a bureaucracy of such size that it can well stifle individual achievement. A competent company president can channel individual entrepreneurial spirit for faster response to new opportunities or threats to the business. In large measure, our individual companies finance their own growth, so are not held back by losing priority to other companies or divisions through requiring corporate financing. What applies to the company applies to the R&D unit associated with it; the opportunity is provided for entrepreneurial effort and, to a large degree, the success of the company depends on it.

Robert Levinson, in his new book *The Decentralized Company,* says that radical decentralization "is not a panacea for an ailing enterprise or a guarantee of business success, but is the concept of management under which humanization, personalization, and maximum profit results are most readily achieved, given a people-sensitive management team and the right set of circumstances."[2] As Jack Goldman observes, we are seeing a lot of entrepreneurial activity in recently formed small companies. Decentralizing our activities, we have sought to capture as much entrepreneurial spirit as possible.

Decentralization is also adaptable to geographic separation and multisite operations. The organization is driven more from the bottom up, as decisions are delegated to lower levels. This tends to increase the responsibility of people at lower levels, giving them a greater sense of involvement in the business, and greater individual opportunities to influence the course of various research activities in company programs. This is a very positive morale factor. Experience demonstrates that the bigger the operation, the more ivory-tower management is apt to be. In the smaller decentralized R&D unit, it is easier for management to mingle with the troops, and so get to know them as individuals, to know what they are up to, and what their real problems are. Strange things can happen when the troops are strangers to management.

Placing more responsibility at lower levels tends to identify and develop managers. And, as we will see, this is an urgent need in decentralized organizations.

Perhaps the greatest advantage of the decentralization of R&D is its integration into the planning and operating team of the individual business unit. When the R&D function is both organizationally and physically part of the operating unit, intracompany communication is greatly facilitated. The R&D people have a better understanding of the business mission and consumer needs and wants. They share many of the same problems as their colleagues, so that communciation is more open and

[2]Robert E. Levinson, *The Decentralized Company.* New York: AMACOM, 1983.

intimate. Successful innovation requires continuous tuning of the entire system, and complete and immediate communication is frequently essential. The understanding resulting from this closer communication results in better project selection. The objectives for R&D activities are more easily established, and, therefore, how to distribute limited resources is easier to decide than in a centralized R&D organization.

The timely solution of technical problems based on practical requirements eliminates overkill and leads to more rapid exploitation of research results. In applying technology, decentralized labs are more effective than centralized ones. The concentration on a particular business segment resulting from the defined mission and the particular technologies required to accomplish the mission frequently permits the decentralized unit to become more knowledgeable than competition that is not so organized, and thus to be more responsive to opportunities.

All types of R&D activity, from the more basic or exploratory to the highly developmental, are working in close proximity and with common goals. This tends to eliminate or at least reduce the "class distinction" which frequently exists between researchers in developmental as opposed to more basic research activities, thus removing many communication problems.

Problems of Decentralized R&D

Now to consider some of the problems of decentralized R&D. There is no question that decentralization involves increased costs, more facilities, services and specialized equipment. It is the price one must be willing to pay to obtain its advantages.

Also, technological innovation today seems to demand a critical mass that contains a sufficient array of specific basic skills, both in R&D and in nontechnical functions. This requirement applies to people and equipment. Some decentralized units of big corporations are as large or larger than many companies, and do not have a problem in meeting this requirement. When the decentralized R&D unit is small, it can have a very limiting effect on the scope of activities that can be undertaken, and thus on the unit's growth. This deficiency is sometimes overcome by contracting for needed resources outside the company, if these resources are required only infrequently and it would be uneconomical to develop in-house competence.

Perhaps the greatest potential difficulty of decentralized R&D is short-term thinking. There may be a strong tendency to pursue more defensive R&D and minimum-risk programs, confined to product-line extensions or relatively minor product improvements. Too much effort may be directed toward supporting the day-to-day efforts of the profit center and R&D may be dominated by strong financial or marketing functions whose overriding interest is in short-term profits. Robert

Levinson points out that this is more of a problem if what he terms pseudo-decentralization into profit centers, rather than truly radical decentralization, has been carried out.

In any event, it is easy to fall into the pitfalls of short-term thinking: for instance, reduced R&D expenditures to preserve or increase near-term profit and resulting product obsolescence. With a necessarily somewhat narrow mission, one's outlook and one's horizons can become very parochial. If, however, one is aware of the problem, steps can be taken to prevent this from happening. Our success in decentralized management depends upon the abilities of the unit manager. The company president or general manager and his management board, which includes the R&D head, are charged with the development of their businesses area for the long term, as well as with its present health and profitability. For the company president to do this, a strong research and development head is essential.

Decentralization requires more managers and this puts greater demands on management development. But, as previously mentioned, the delegation of decision-making power to lower levels in the decentralized unit helps to identify and develop the required management talent.

Pulling together the collective strengths of the corporation to tackle a major problem is sometimes an urgent necessity. In a decentralized organization such as ours, that is a harder problem to deal with. The required resources may be available within the corporation, but it is difficult, and sometimes virtually impossible, to bring the full strength of the corporation to bear on the problem.

Decentralization increases interunit-communication problems, and thus works against interunit cooperation. While there may be a willingness to help another unit, limited R&D resources frequently make this difficult. There is not the same flexibility and versatility in mobilizing resources that one enjoys with a central laboratory. There is always the possibility that duplication of R&D efforts will take place due to a lack of adequate communication or an overlapping of units' interests. But in my experience, this is a much overrated problem, and has certainly not presented difficulties at Johnson & Johnson. And sometimes, of course, duplicate efforts should be encouraged.

Decentralized units, more closely tied to somewhat narrower interests by their mission, may not develop as broad contacts in the scientific and technical community outside the company as is desirable. This can result in their being less effective in evaluating and incorporating new technology, and there is the danger of their resistance to the intrusion of new ideas from the outside.

In a completely decentralized organization, R&D reports to the individual decentralized units, and thus does not have the same status in the corporation as a corporate lab reporting to senior corporate management. R&D's influence in the corporation as a whole, may not, therefore, be as great. The decentralized lab may be less visible from outside, and its individual scientists may feel disadvantaged by this. If the scope of the decentralized unit appears too narrow in terms of resources, individuals may perceive very limited horizons and it may, therefore, be harder to recruit really top scientists. The environment may not be attractive to scientists who have acquired highly specialized skills and want to capitalize on them.

The decentralized lab, because of its more limited scope, is subject to fire-fighting type technical-service demands and to competitive pressures. Profit problems may cause difficulties in maintaining the continuity of programs, and produce the so-called yo-yo effect of starting and stopping projects.

The Mixed Mode

In view of this catalog of advantages and disadvantages, it comes as no surprise that the most common pattern for companies large enough to consider alternatives of centralization and decentralization is to choose a mixed mode, employing a central or corporate lab for longer-range, higher-risk research, and decentralizing all other R&D in an attempt to reap the benefit of both systems. The 3M Company has carried this one step further and has a three-tier research organization. The central lab handles long-range pioneering programs, with a time span of ten years or more in the future. The sector labs, of which I understand there are four, have a time frame of five to ten years and a goal of developing and expanding strong technology bases in areas of particular interest to their sectors. The traditional divisional labs remain responsible for serving the divisions' market needs, providing new products and process improvements to serve customers effectively.

There are a variety of hybrid structures with new blends of decentralization and corporate surveillance to take advantage of the ability to react quickly, but with headquarters becoming more assertive in strategic planning, resource allocation, and deployment of people. In Johnson & Johnson we are very careful about providing direction and support for individual operating units. "I'm from corporate and I'm here to help you" often reminds our managers of promises like, "The check is in the mail," and "I'll still love you in the morning." We believe in decentralization and not just on an organization chart, which is meaningless unless responsibility is given to the decentralized unit. Ours are not merely profit centers, but business-development units, and in order to take care of their long-range interests, we have felt it essential that they control their own R&D activities.

Otherwise the management cannot be expected to accept this responsibility. We are thus asking a great deal from the R&D unit head or vice president: his function must be integrated as fully as possible into the business, and, at the same time, he must remain fully cognizant of the new science and technology that may affect the business. This executive must champion R&D programs which may not be fully appreciated by colleagues in management because of the newness of the technology.

We have, over the past few years, inaugurated some activities designed to assist the decentralized units in carrying out their role, particularly as related to new science and technology. The Corporate Office of Science and Technology, for which I am responsible, was established for this purpose. It makes me a very rare bird, one of unusual plumage in our company, because we have a very small corporate staff. I hope it isn't such a rare bird that it is an endangered species. We are responsible for assisting the decentralized units to keep up with the ever-widening knowledge base in science, in some areas very accurately described as revolutionary, and thus help them to upgrade their internal scientific competence. This is being done by bringing in academicians and other outsiders for seminars, and by sponsoring research activities in the universities and getting our people involved with those activities. We are constantly on the lookout for external scientific and technological resources applicable to our present and future business interests, and we assist the operating companies in exploiting these. We act as a catalyst to promote cooperation among the companies. We are generally more aware of the interests of the various affiliates than they are of each other's interests.

Another responsibility is to identify corporate opportunities in new science and technology which may fall outside of our present company interests and which no individual company might be aware of. We are also coordinating an outside advisory committee to help keep us alert to what is going on beyond the confines of Johnson & Johnson. We have formed a development company, which has made equity investments in com- panies whose technologies are of interest. We are not classic venture capitalists interested in making money, even though we don't mind doing so in those investments; but in this way we can keep up with many new developments in science and technology and provide our companies with additional potential sources of new products.

We have created ad hoc groups to carry out R&D activities in specific areas of interest to more than one company, either as a center of technology within one company, or as a stand-alone unit. Although organized under corporate auspices, the groups are funded by individual companies.

So we, like everyone else, are struggling with how best to keep up with science and technology, and support longer-range activities while capitalizing on immediate opportunities. Management's attitudes toward organization of R&D should be permissive, so that ad hoc arrangements for particular needs or special situations may be made. The adequacy of the existing organization should be continuously challenged.

Most of the disadvantages of either a decentralized or centralized system can be dealt with, and the trick is to decide which will be easier to overcome, based on a company's particular character and objectives. Many choose some sort of hybrid structure in order to balance long- and short-term interests. Management can prepare the corporation for the fruits of research by assuring a common understanding of goals, so that research activities are effectively integrated into the business. The marketing-research interface is particularly critical; each party must be schooled to understand the other, and both must understand their customer.

Echoing what others have said, I do not feel the organization per se is the key factor. The most important factor in the effectiveness of R&D is people, and no form of organization can substitute for competent personnel. With the right people, any form of organization will succeed, but a poor form of organization can make life unnecessarily complicated for them.

Another Perspective

Dr. Robert E. Wilson, Senior Vice President and Director, Heidrick and Stuggles, who chaired the session on "Organizing for R&D," offered these observations in introducing the session:

Whether to organize R&D in a given company as a centralized or decentralized function is often a difficult question. The choice sometimes yields results not as successful as desired. Some companies have, in fact, gone back and forth between the two organization modes more than once.

Several factors influence the organization of R&D groups and their relationships with other parts of the corporation. The more important ones include:

- The company's philosophy,
- The contribution desired from R&D at a given time: whether emphasis is on new products, new processes or new technology,
- The perception of R&D by the board of directors and other members of top management,
- The personalities and technical competence of the members of top management; their understanding of R&D; and the degree of their comfort with alternative types of organization,
- The size and composition of R&D organization, the strength of its leadership, the diversity of the technologies in which the company is involved, geographical distribution of R&D facilities, and the methods used by the company for utilizing R&D results.

Since centralized and decentralized modes each have advantages, the decision should not be made arbitrarily, but should be based on careful consideration of all relevant factors.

In general, a centralized approach provides for better technology transfer within the R&D organization and reduces duplication of effort. A centralized mode also usually permits a better response to long-term corporate objectives and more effective direction and coordination. A centralized mode sometimes enables the firm to attract a higher quality staff; this is particularly true of the chief technical officer. On the negative side, technology transfer to operating groups is often difficult.

A decentralized approach is frequently desirable when the company is involved with a high number of different technologies. Response times are often reduced, and it is possible to focus more effectively on specific projects with serious time limitations. On the negative side, cross-fertilization among technical specialists is not as likely; vision may be restricted; and parochialism may develop.

Within these two modes, a variety of organizations exist. The most common centralized form receives its direction from a corporate officer, generally identified as the chief technical officer, who most often reports to the CEO. In this type of organization, most, if not all, of the technical activity of the company (sometimes including corporate engineering) reports to this position.

In the typical decentralized organization, R&D units are usually assigned to divisions or other operating groups, generally reporting to the group general managers. The company may or may not have a corporate R&D group. When a corporate group exists, a dotted-line relationship with the divisional R&D units is common. Wide variations of these models exist, of course, reflecting the specific requirements of a given company.

Since either organization mode can be successful, emphasis should be placed on the development of a technical capability that promotes a cooperative spirit and encourages a high incidence of transfer of personnel and technology between appropriate units of the organization.

Chapter 10
Internal Ventures—Perspective and Impact

A.B. Cohen
Director of Research, Electronics, Photosystems
 and Electronic Products Department
E.I. du Pont de Nemours and Company

Organizing internal ventures—new businesses within an established company—is perhaps the ultimate challenge to R&D. At times, it can be quite frustrating, particularly when the venture is based on highly innovative technology but misses its mark because it lacks equally imaginative market planning. Yet when it is right, no R&D investment pays back a greater return to the parent company. And for the managers who accept this challenge, there can be no better learning experience—or more fun.

Among the dozens of internal ventures in Du Pont over the past 30 years, nowhere has the impact on restructuring a business been greater than in the Photo Products Department. For that reason I thought it would be most interesting to focus on that experience, and to share some of the lessons we learned. But first, a brief review of the R&D environment from which we launch new ventures.

The R&D Environment

R&D is largely decentralized within seven industrial departments. Each functions like an independent company in organizing and allocating R&D resources to meet specific business needs.

Most new ventures in Du Pont originate within industrial departments. However, the centralized Development Division was set up to initiate ventures that lie outside the business scope or expertise of existing industrial departments. Some of these corporate ventures have provided these departments with attractive opportunities for diversification and growth.

Photo Products' business scope is defined as "materials and systems for recording, retrieving and display of information." The worldwide information explosion has made fast-changing industries like printing,

electronics and medical diagnostics attractive targets for growth and diversification. With a charter this broad, we made a major commitment to long-range research in some unconventional areas of technology to provide the seeds for new ventures. These exploratory research programs often precede the formal ventures by five or ten years. They have provided a progressive hierarchy of innovative technology on which to draw.

Photopolymers have been a source for many ventures. They are light-sensitive plastics that can be precisely modified for specific uses by exposing them to light through a photographic mask. Our basic solid-state research has also provided unique magnetic and electronic technologies for new ventures.

In budgeting for R&D, we try to assure a healthy balance between products with incremental improvements, which are needed to support today's businesses, and novel products that are aimed at creating new market opportunities. For many of today's dynamic industries, we have found it advantageous to develop the product concurrently with the other parts of the system they are to fit into. For example, by developing a consumable film, processing chemicals, and equipment as an integrated technology package, the proposed commercial system can be optimized to better fulfill customer needs. As a consequence, we end up with a turnkey system which greatly speeds up commercial introduction. Where such a system involves a major commitment in new resources, or is aimed at a totally new area of business, setting up an internal venture is considered.

The Anatomy of an Internal Venture

Interest in internal ventures has been spurred by the astonishing success of many high-risk independent ventures. Often, these were started up by a lone entrepreneur with few resources other than unique ideas and boundless energy and determination. That's a hard act to follow, but it is a good model to start with.

The internal venture is set up as a specialized group within the parent organization. It functions like a small independent business, with full responsibility for developing manufacturing and marketing the proposed new systems. Integration of these three functions within a tightly knit organization usually creates an exciting environment for managing change. This atmosphere is highly conducive to generating new ideas and taking risks. It encourages researchers to seek truly innovative products with long-term impact, rather than those dictated by need for fast payback.

Both internal ventures and established businesses appear to have similar functional organizations. In a venture, however, the technical, marketing and manufacturing managers are much more focused on their common goal than on their specific functions. They are development oriented rather than operations oriented. Their major mission is to create a new business, not to run one.

Since development needs can change quickly, particularly in a high-tech venture, all the functional managers must be fully involved in day-to-day venture management. Midcourse corrections are frequently needed, and decisions to make them must be well coordinated and promptly executed.

Some Examples

In the 1950's, Photo Products was the smallest department in Du Pont. It was also one of the least profitable. We marketed a fairly conventional line of photographic films for professional and industrial markets.

Marketing had recommended development of a totally synthetic film base to improve our competitive position in the cine film business. The resulting synthetic polyester film proved to be much stronger and more stable than existing cellulosic films, but less easy to splice. It did turn out to be a great success, but not in the cine area, where ease of splicing is important. Fortuitously, we had selected the right product but the wrong market. We made a quick mid-course correction. Automatic processing of photographic films was just getting underway. Our strong synthetic film withstood the rough machine handling much better than cellulosic films. It gave us a competitive edge which greatly expanded our X-ray and graphic arts film businesses.

As I indicated earlier, photopolymers have been a fertile technology base for many new ventures. Our first photopolymer venture was aimed at replacing engraved metal printing plates by photosensitive plastic printing plates. The photopolymer process is faster, less expensive, and safer. Various types of photopolymer printing plates are now widely used throughout the world. One spinoff from this versatile technology resulted in a photographic process for making flexographic printing plates. They replaced lower quality plates made by a laborious rubber-molding process. There were also some quite different spinoffs.

The most successful photopolymer ventures were based on photosensitive films that can be thermally laminated to metal or paper. One of these novel systems revolutionized the way printed circuits for computers are fabricated. These multilayered circuits pack a lot of circuitry in a little space. Photopolymer films provided the high reliability they needed.

A related system led to a new venture based on a sophisticated custom color proofing system for lithography. The speed and accuracy of this multicolor system in simulating press prints at low cost have made it a worldwide standard for color printing.

Other internal ventures in Photo Products led to chromium-based magnetic tapes, which are almost universally used for video recording and our highly successful automatic clinical analyzer, which is computer controlled for selecting and running up to 64 diagnostic tests.

These ventures were major commitments. They involved not only new technology, but also different manufacturing processes and unfamiliar markets. We could have chosen lesser goals. They would have involved much less risk, but they would also have offered much less opportunity. We decided to go for broke! In retrospect, that was a wise decision. The most profitable and fastest growing ventures proved to be those where we had taken the greatest risk.

Photo Products has diversified considerably. We are still heavily involved in photosystems. However, we have focused on those segments of the professional photographic business in which we have been able to develop a leadership position because of technical innovations like our polyster film base. Overall, Photo Products today is one of the most specialized high-technology departments in Du Pont. It has also grown into one of Du Pont's largest and most profitable industrial departments.

Of eleven new major product lines introduced between 1960 and the present, nine are a result of internal venture developments. The other two were external acquisitions. These ventures are focused on some of the highest growth areas in today's industrial scene.

A Few Pointers

We have found some ways to reduce risk and increase chance of success. One of the first requirements, of course, is selecting a viable concept for the proposed new business. This depends on accurately identifying the *real* market need and an innovative way to fill that need. People usually identify needs in terms of what already exists—that is why traditional market research often fails in high-tech forecasting. A successful forecaster must have sufficient insight to interpret needs in terms of what might be, rather than just what is.

But even where the need is real and the timing right, the venture can still fail if the product concept is too complicated, too hazardous, or too costly to fit its market environment. Too often, we design tomorrow's products to fill yesterday's needs.

Financing a new venture is long-term investment for the future. Preferably it should be budgeted out of corporate funds. Otherwise it is likely to be too sensitive to the economic needs of the current business and aim only at short-range objectives.

In organizing a venture, it is just as important to find the right venture manager as it is to find the right ideas. The venture manager must be an entrepreneur capable of operating a total business and willing to assume the risks of the venture. Also, at times, the person must be as much an artist as a scientist or business manager, employing innovative solutions to problems and encouraging creativity in the venture group. The venture manager must be involved in every step of the product cycle: manufacturing, marketing and research. The ability to understand the intimate interaction of these functions, and to communicate their significance is a key to the success of the venture. Above all, the manager must be decisive. The worst decision in a fast-moving venture is indecision.

Last, but certainly not least, is the venture staff itself. It is often necessary to go outside the parent company for specific skills. Persons selected for ventures must not only be innovative and experienced, but they must be real team players. They will be more effective if they are comfortable with change, since changes occur frequently in highly charged ventures.

As Time Goes By

This final section might be subtitled: "What have you done for me lately?" In time, even the most successful new venture becomes an old venture. High-tech businesses, particularly electronics businesses, have short life cycles. If they are to continue to grow, they must be willing to undertake new internal ventures, even while the recently established businesses are still healthy and growing.

In our electronic businesses, we currently have about a half dozen such major ventures. The basic R&D for many of these new internal ventures was started, in many cases, even before the old venture was commercialized. Let me give two examples.

I talked earlier about an internal venture that had resulted in a revolutionary new method for making printed circuits. That system was introduced in 1968 under the name of Riston[r]. It is widely used by computer manufacturers throughout the world and is still growing faster than the economy as a whole. It has been improved by many evolutionary changes, but at the same time we have been planning a totally new system that again involves revolutionary changes.

This new integrated system involves a totally new type of photopolymer film. It also provides a much higher level of automation and control of key process variables that affect process reliability and fabrication costs. For example, when fully implemented, it will require only two operators instead of nine, and eliminate the need for the traditional clean room used in microelectronics.

For still longer range developments in electronics, we have set up a multiventure group that we call Advanced Electronics Systems. It involves a major commitment to long-term growth and further diversification. This group is currently exploring totally new methods for fabricating printed circuits and electronic components that will be needed for the next generation of high-capacity miniature computers.

Our Advanced Electronics Group has its own market planning group made up of innovative scientists who also understand the marketplace. They have tried to fit our unique technical capabilities to future market needs of electronics in the next decade. We hope the new internal ventures we are just launching will play a major role in this next revolution.[1]

---

[1]Since this talk was presented, Du Pont has announced a reorganization of several industrial departments to better reflect current business and technology alignments. The PhotoProducts Department has become the Photosystems and Electronic Products Department. The biomedical portions of Photo Products are part of a new Biomedical Department.

Chapter 11
R&D in the Context of the Whole Organization

Edward B. Roberts
David Sarnoff Professor of the Management
   of Technology and Chairman,
MIT Technology and Health Management Group

There are two purposes in organizing. One is to accomplish a myriad of individual tasks efficiently and effectively. The second is to integrate multiple tasks in order to achieve the goals of the institution as a whole. These two orientations are very different; and when we focus upon research and development, they correspond to two major gaps that exist within the R&D environment.

At the level of the individual task of performing R&D, the fundamental problem relates to getting the right sets of inputs into the technical organization to guide its direction and content. As for integration, the problem is to get the appropriate transfer of R&D results to the commercializing divisions of the company—into manufacturing and to the marketplace—which, of course, provide the funds to support not just R&D but the business as a whole.

Not accidentally, the MIT Master's Degree program in Management of Technology aims at taking technically trained and technically experienced people in their mid-careers and giving them the specialized management training and insights to help them not only to lead technical organizations, but to link these organizations to the rest of the corporation.

Inputs

It appears to me that several kinds of inputs are needed for effective R&D. One is information. With respect to information, I think that the problem of integrating R&D into the rest of the firm begins with inappropriate planning of research and development.

Technology planning within the corporation is needed to answer questions at three quite different levels: First, how does one link the technological strengths of the R&D organization with the markets and the distribution capabilities of the firm to effect overall strategic choice of the corporation? That is a very broad-based macro-strategic planning issue.

Second, how should R&D resources already in place be allocated among major product lines and major product areas—those that exist today and those that might exist in the future?

Third is a very different kind of technology-planning problem: What specific R&D product and process projects should be undertaken and how much money and time should be allocated for these individual tasks?

In my opinion, technology-planning activities in all three of these areas are ineffectively carried out by most corporations. Little or no attention is paid to the macrotechnological planning activities at all. If planning is carried out, it is entirely at the level of individual projects, selection, scheduling and the like.

At a minimum, R&D and marketing organizations need close ties. And this relates not just to the planning functions, but to all of the rest of the major undertakings of a technical organization. One recent study indicated that under conditions of harmonious relationships between R&D and marketing, 50 percent of the new product projects met with complete commercial success. And that may be the maximum that one could hope to expect. The same study indicated that under conditions of severe disharmony in relationships between marketing and R&D, only 10 percent of the new project developments achieved complete commercial success. Thus, the issues involved in linkages at the informational level are very critical.

Key Roles

Another key input is skills—the organization's staffing needs to reflect a mix of the key roles that are necessary to bring the proper inputs into the organization and then have the proper actions take place. Jack Goldman commented on the need for assurance of the highest quality of personnel (page 7). This quality should not be limited to a single set of skills; a multidimensional set is really needed. For the steady and successful generation and implementation of innovative activities, five roles have to be played within the organization, not all of them by the R&D unit.

First is the role everybody thinks about with respect to R&D: generating ideas. Next is the entrepreneurial role. It is inadequate to point out that lots of entrepreneurship is going on in new firms around Route 128. But the existence of entrepreneurship in small companies is no excuse for its absence in large companies. Instead, we have to identify the means for large firms to have entrepreneurship present and strongly represented within the technical and marketing organizations that are trying to create new product lines and new processes.

The third role is that of gatekeeping: The process of bringing in technical information from outside sources as well as from the market. Those information-transfer people are critical to obtaining both effective inputs to and integration of a technical organization.

Fourth is the project manager role, quite different from the roles already outlined. It is not the same as coming up with an idea or championing an idea. Rather its essence is bringing together people and myriad resources, and coping with tight schedules, budgets, and so on. Like the other critical roles, that of program manager has to be identified and supported in the corporate structure.

The final role—the role that especially those in senior technical management and, even more appropriately, senior general management positions should seek to fulfill—is that of sponsor. Sponsors provide protection, facilitation, encouragement; provide the corporate culture and environment and support within which the rest of these activities take place, even though they may not be directly involved in the projects themselves.

We have carried out studies in a large number of corporate organizations, and whenever we find deficiencies in the filling of any one of these roles, we find major problems in whether R&D is appropriately directed, is moving forward appropriately, and is being implemented appropriately in the marketplace.

The next necessary input comes from the user. It is commonplace to say that one needs to pay attention to markets and to get information from customers as to what they want, so as to target technology developments to the customer. But that is not the best that users inputs can provide. In a large number of industries, innovative users can be counted on not just for information but for finished new product development. If one associates with innovative users in the right industries, one can bring completely implemented innovations into the firm at the point of final product engineering or manufacturing engineering, and skip the stages of early research and development. Eric Von Hippel, one of my colleagues at MIT, has found in the areas of scientific instruments, electronic assembly, and other industrial goods, that the user can be counted on to be the primary supplier of innovative final products to the company that is alert and is concerned about these inputs.

What does that say about organization? If one can find shortcuts for internal R&D by appropriate relationships with the customer, then that suggests something about how to organize not just the technical staff, but the marketing and sales organizations as well, to provide the opportunities for that linkage to the customers, to provide appropriate incentives, to bring information and results back from the customer, and to create very different kinds of linkage structures from those most corporations have formally implemented.

So both inputs from within and inputs from without are necessary.

Transfer

The second problem I identified at the outset is that effective organization is also needed to cause the results of R&D to be appropriately transferred. Dr. Goldman's comment that the greatest risk management faces is in coping with the results of successful R&D is very important. Technically successful R&D, especially if it embraces radical innovation, is very likely to pose major problems of linkages with the rest of the firm, problems with which the rest of the firm is unprepared to deal. The successful new venture R&D project often encounters a corporate budgeting process that cannot deal with the magnitude of millions of dollars of funds necessary for manufacturing implementation or for large-scale market implementation. In these circumstances, companies have done a terrific job of R&D—and a terrible job of managing the innovation process overall.

Critical Linkages

Here are some of the critical linkages to the rest of the firm necessary for successful transfer.

First is manufacturing acceptance: Whatever is coming out of R&D, whether new or improved product, or new or improved process, change must show up first in the manufacturing organization. Whether the manufacturing organization is the link to the market, or is itself the purchaser or absorber of the innovation, manufacturing ties to R&D are critical, but tend to be very weak in many corporations. This problem especially exists where research and development laboratories are centralized, or where new venture groups are independent of the manufacturing divisions of the company. In these instances, manufacturing acceptance is often the first barrier; unless it is surmounted, a new R&D development will not find its way to the marketplace.

Beyond the manufacturing sector, the marketing and sales people have to contribute as well. They should have participated in earlier stages of planning. They should have been aware at some stage of what is likely to come out of the R&D organization. They cannot be confronted abruptly with R&D results and be expected to react with enthusiasm and move products forward in the market.

Finally, a part of the organization frequently ignored, yet vital, especially in the area of industrial goods, is the field-service organization. What is going to be required of the field-service people to handle the distribution and maintenance of the product in the field is inadequately considered or overlooked during the early planning stages of R&D activity. That hurts both the likelihood and success of new product innovation.

One approach to ensure proper linkage is to use product teams. DuPont uses new-venture product teams (pp. 39-41). So does the 3M Corporation. The idea is to bring representatives from separate functional groups into a single product-team organization, integrating contributors within a group that has life-cycle commitment to moving an idea forward toward the market and use by customers, perhaps shifting emphasis among key players in that team as a project moves from stage to stage. It is essential to have an integrated team from the outset. This requires pulling team members away from their respective functional bases. The potential problem in doing so is that the people who have gone off to do their own thing on a product team become alienated from those who stay behind within the functional groups that often control the major resources of the firm. So, although the product team concept is worth considering, it will not necessarily work in all firms.

Changed Procedures

Another means to consider for coping with the transfer issue is to build bridges to the commercial units by changes of procedures within the organization, rather than changes of organization structure. To the extent that they work, procedural changes are inexpensive and easy to implement. Examples include joint planning of R&D programs, at least between R&D and marketing people, if not with other functional areas; joint staffing of projects, especially during the immediate pre- and post-project transfer stage and especially between R&D and manufacturing; and joint appraisal of results by all of the functional areas that have been involved.

The last is very easy to undertake, but has to be done very sensitively. From the viewpoint of generating useful information, the best time to carry out joint appraisal of results is when failure has occurred. Then there is something objective to look at to try to determine what can be learned. But that is the most dangerous time to carry out joint appraisal; joint appraisal of a failure becomes an opportunity for fingerpointing and mutual blame giving.

What about joint appraisal of a successful project? Many say that it is unnecessary. Why bother if the battle has been won? Yet that is the time when available information can be gathered in an environment of goodwill and good feelings. Carrying out joint appraisal of successfully developed and implemented projects can well strengthen linkages among R&D, marketing and manufacturing, and may yield enough goodwill to tide the organization over failed projects.

The establishment of human bridges also helps to cope with transfer issues. Informal contacts inevitably turn out to be the base for interorganizational linkages that really matter. My MIT colleague, Thomas Allen, has found that the bulk of the critical inputs and product-development activities comes from face-to-face contacts among individuals, contacts that are largely unscheduled and arise out of factors relating to physical space and how laboratories are laid out, past project identification and relationships, neighborly relationships outside the organization, and so on. Anything that can be done to stimulate informal contacts among different parts of the organization is likely to be helpful, both on the input side and on the transfer-of-results side.

Formal meetings, as much as people may like or dislike them, are also useful, especially meetings that turn out to be internal promotional affairs, in which one organization reports on what it has been doing, and on the kind of capability it has.

The 3M Corporation, for example, holds a proprietary company fair, open only to company people, at which there are presentations of technical papers, exhibits and demonstrations of projects and prototypes. The fair enables the rest of the people in the company to begin to learn about what is taking place in other divisions or laboratories. This kind of formal meeting structure does an enormous amount to foster communication, and to stimulate the identification of capability and of needs throughout the firm.

The Monsanto Company uses what it calls the Monsanto Technical Community to bring together technical people, trained in similar disciplines but employed in different divisions of the firm. It convenes these people in formal meetings, encouraging them to exchange ideas.

In this fashion, appropriately structured formal meetings, with a bit of creativity devoted to the agenda, the purpose, and the mechanism employed, may go a long way to provide the kinds of integrated linkages that otherwise may be lacking in some very large and geographically dispersed corporations.

Rotation programs, not practiced frequently enough by American corporations but popular in Japan, can also be fruitful. Japanese organizations assume that the best course of development for the capable individual is lateral rotation across major functional areas of the firm before upward advancement takes place. An individual progressing well in a Japanese company moves from R&D into marketing, then into manufacturing, and then perhaps back into R&D at a higher level. That is seldom the kind of progress that American firms find appropriate. Yet one knows instinctively what kinds of insights, bridge building, and relationships would flower over the long run by greater adoption of rotation programs. They would be desirable even if rotation were limited to between research and separate development or engineering groups, or between R&D groups and manufacturing engineering groups, or between R&D groups and field-service support groups. Such programs would do an enormous amount to change the nature of the inputs to the R&D program, and the ability later on to transfer successfully the results of R&D.

The concept of liaison personnel between organizations is also intriguing. I call them market gatekeepers: people from the technical organization who try to relate to the product and market areas. At one time, Robert Charpie, as vice president of technology for Union Carbide, had a small group of highly competent people whose task was to work themselves out of a job within two years by finding ways of linking their own talents to market and technical opportunities that could assist the Union Carbide Company to move forward in new areas of product and business development. This approach, emphasizing a degree of aggressiveness by the market gatekeeper, is akin to some programs today for stimulating entrepreneurship in large companies.

Another device to be considered is the joint problem-solving meeting. How often is one asked to sit down with colleagues in another part of the firm to let them explain their difficulties, as opposed to having them describe their successes or their great virtues? When people are called together to listen to problems in the attempt to stimulate idea generation, it often happens that the ideas that emerge contribute not just to the initially stated problems, but may very well help in solving other problems.

Organizational Changes

The final area to consider for facilitating transfer of R&D results to commercialization consists of organizational changes and organizational bridges. The reason organizational bridges are discussed last, instead of first, is that they are the toughest to create and implement in an organization. It is much easier to alter procedures, it is much easier to try to build human bridges across groups, than it is to change organizational structure.

The first approach, specialized transfer groups, is one that executives in process industries will quickly realize they follow when important new processes, developed by others, are to be introduced in their companies. If they get a license for a process, they expect that the licensor will not just send equipment and documentation, but also capable people who can train others, who can install that equipment, who can get the plant up and functioning.

But how often do these same executives consider creating a specialized transfer group if the issue is internal transfer of what might become the next most significant business for the company, the transfer from the laboratory to the manufacturing plant or from the laboratory to the marketplace? Senior managers are likely to say: 'We can't spare the superstars of the technical organization to spend time in manufacturing, or to support field marketing or distribution personnel. We need them back in R&D.''

For excellent examples of how specialized teams are employed for external transfer, look at any of the chemical engineering process companies, or look at how Pilkington Glass has proceeded to install float-glass plants all over the world both for company-owned plants and for customers it licenses. These approaches may suggest sound internal transfer mechanisms when the product opportunities are significant enough.

A second organizational approach is to employ an "integrator," the person whose job it is to straddle more than one organization, to bridge the no-man's land between R&D and marketing. It is a job that is uncomfortable at the least, and often very difficult. People are quickly fired—or disappear from jobs as integrators. But those who succeed at it usually move very quickly up the organizational hierarchy because they are identified as people who not only can straddle organizations, but can also cope with the political sensitivities of multiple groups within the firm.

Then there is the approach described by Dr. Cohen of DuPont: the internal venture team.

Corporate Venture Strategies

A variety of corporate venture strategies can be considered by companies that are concerned with developing new approaches and new product lines, and with emphasizing entrepreneurship. As is shown, these strategies form a spectrum; a company is not limited to the extreme end of internal ventures if it wishes to build new and diverse businesses. That end of the spectrum requires the highest degree of corporate involvement and the highest degree of corporate willingness to accept risk.

It is a wonderful place to be if the corporate attitude is supportive.

SPECTRUM OF VENTURE STRATEGIES

Venture Capital	Venture Nurturing	Venture Spin-off	New Style Joint Ventures	Venture Merging & Melding	Internal Ventures
Low Involvement					High Involvement

Required Corporate Involvement ⟶

But there are other options: For instance, at the other extreme of the spectrum, venture-capital investments in outside firms, for the purpose of gaining windows on technology and on new market opportunities, or any other point on the spectrum.[1] For example, an integration of strengths of large companies and small companies may through new forms of joint ventures be a better strategy to follow for both the large and the small. The large company has resources in manufacturing, in distribution and in finance that the small company can not hope to duplicate unless it also becomes a large company. The small company may, in fact, be at the leading edge of certain advanced-technology areas. It

may have more implicit entrepreneurial energy and commitment, and almost certainly has more flexibility of choice and implementation. But possessing entrepreneurial skills, even possessing advanced technology, even having great flexibility, are not enough to cause small companies to be successful. They somehow have to be able to acquire the capital, manufacturing and marketing resources to enable that entrepreneurship to be implemented in the marketplace.

So it is well to consider new forms of linkages between the large firm and the small. On my spectrum, this is midway between spending a little money and spending a lot, which is entailed by DuPont's internal venture program. A large firm may well be able to consider ways of integrating internal R&D and R&D drawn from the small independent company.

[1] For additional information, see Edward B. Roberts, "New Ventures for Corporate Growth." *Harvard Business Review,* July-August, 1980.

Chapter 12
Questions and Answers

Question for Dr. Thomas and Dr. Fuller: How does one utilize scientific advisory groups in centralized and decentralized organizations? And how does one communicate with these groups?

DR. THOMAS: At Kodak, it is fairly simple. We have an organized structure for managing all the routine functions of the laboratory, and, of course, a hierarchical system for technical direction. But we emphasize the importance of the dual ladder. It is extremely important in a research operation to be able to reward top performers who are perhaps not well suited for management but who are extremely competent or creative or are real technical spearheads. As these people progress, as they move up the dual ladder and become recognized as technical experts, we add them to the Scientific and Technical Advisory Committee.

The committee meets regularly with me every other week. The meetings may have no structure whatsoever; we may just go around the table and see what is on people's minds, or the participants may get specific assignments. For example, I have a list of topics given to me by the committee. These topics, in the view of these top technical people, represent the principal unsolved but important technical problems facing Eastman Kodak Company for the next few years. By virtue of close working relationships with many of the scientists in the laboratory, the members of the committee have a somewhat different relationship with the lab community from management's.

Thus, there are two separate channels for getting new scientific and technical issues on the table. The committee provides a much-needed and welcome forum for the people on the technical side of the dual ladder to have direct access to management and to have influence on R&D policies and decisions. It was amazing to me that, once we had set up the committee, after its members had gotten all the frustrations that had built up over the years off their chests, how harmonious the relationship between the committee and management turned out to be within about six months.

DR. FULLER: I have interpreted the question to mean our scientific advisory board of people outside the company, because we do not have a committee similar to the one that was just talked about. Only recently, we copied what I guess many smaller companies are doing to get outside scientific advice. The whole purpose of our outside group is to guide our activities in the new fields of biotechnology and molecular biology, where we have many activities under way in the various parts of the company, but where we still are not completely satisfied that we have approached these fields as we should as a corporation. So we simply collected some outside talent to advise us.

Question for Dr. Cohen: Can you tell us how to find or develop the venture managers that you talked about?

DR. COHEN: With great difficulty. Entrepreneurial types, as has been already stated, are not easy to attract to large companies. Usually they are much more comfortable setting up their own companies. So we really concentrate on developing people from within. The kinds of things we look for are not so much scientific ability, or even management ability, in the traditional sense. Most companies are very comfortable with innovators who innovate and managers who manage, but they are still not very comfortable with innovative managers. The people who are attractive candidates for venture-manager positions have certain abilities: They are good problem solvers; they have broad interests; and, in a technology sense, they do not feel locked into what they did in graduate school, but are prepared to get into chemistry, physics or engineering, even though they may have no specific training in the discipline in question.

The other quality that is very important is understanding the marketplace and interrelationship between a need and a product. In our view, inventions do not come out of the laboratory, but are conceived in the marketplace as a result of seeing what the problems are, trying to interpret them, and responding to them. There are some people who do this well, and over the years we have identified such people, and we have built up a pretty good team. These are the people who will become the best types of venture managers.

Question for Dr. Fuller: In the transfer of technology, is it desirable to transfer people from research perhaps through the development stages, along with a given project?

DR. FULLER: That is not a big issue if the organization is decentralized as ours is. We do not have the problem of bringing somebody from a central area into an operating unit. The key people are already in the unit, and I think that is one of the advantages of the decentralized system.

Question for Dr. Thomas: Do you permit duplication of research programs in your foreign laboratories?

DR. THOMAS: Yes, we have extensive participation by the foreign laboratories in laying out general objectives and plans. There is deliberately some overlap in activities, although obviously we try not to structure programs that are exactly the same in two places. It is hard to give quantitative rules for how much overlap there ought to be, but there ought to be some.

Question for Dr. Cohen: What is the funding process for the internal venture? What is the selection process?

DR. COHEN: During the 1960's and 1970's, there was a fairly formal structure in DuPont, and a lot of the ventures were corporate supported. One submitted a proposal for a new venture, and, if accepted, it received a commitment of corporate funds. That practice, I indicated earlier, tended to insulate the venture from the day-to-day pressures of the existing business. Most of the ventures I talked about—at least those now under way in our department—are being financed from departmental funds. To be sure, they are insulated from the smaller profit centers. The allocation is on an annual basis; sometimes it is an even longer-term commitment. The venture I mentioned last, for example, is a very large, mutimillion-dollar venture, and it has an annual budget that is supported by departmental funds.

Question for Dr. Thomas: How are your labs funded? By corporate? By the division? Or do you have clients in the corporation whom you charge?

DR. THOMAS: All the budget for the corporate laboratory comes directly from corporate funds. We participate in the budgeting process, but ultimately the funds are given by the chairman of the board. We are not part, of course, of any of the operating divisions. But I would have to say that the Photographic Division, which makes up abut 75 percent of the company, has a strong interest in our performing certain kinds of tasks for it. We take that division very seriously.

Question for Dr. Roberts: You mentioned that problems start with poor technology planning. Can you give us any clues as to how to improve technology plans?

DR. ROBERTS: Technology planning is the most infantile of the planning areas; the most mature is financial planning. And that may be at the root of many companies' problems. They have a lot of financial planning taking place without relation to technical programs, technical directions, and technical opportunities.

But a variety of new technology-planning techniques are emerging. The use of traditional S-curve analogies, for instance, is useful to evaluate where an organization stands in various stages of technology.[1] Other more significant methods are becoming available. For example, it is possible today to put together teams of technical and marketing people to do technology-planning unit analysis, whereby the team will attempt to appraise the technical skills base of an organization and to align that skills base against the company's market areas. Think of a matrix on the vertical scale of which are listed technology skills and, on the horizontal scale, the markets to which they are applied. An analysis of that sort can identify for a company the areas where technical skills that it possesses are being applied to particular markets, but are not being applied to other markets. That is one easy way to identify new business-development possibilities. And the analysis can run both ways.

But perhaps the simplest place to start in technology planning—and I must observe that most companies need to start at the simplest place because they have not done anything yet—might be to look at one's product lines and to make competitive profiles of them. What are the primary dimensions along which a product's performance should be appraised? Who are the competitors for that product, and how do their performance characteristics stack up against one's own company's? This uncovering of product strengths and deficiencies points to simple program and project development areas.

I think that the literature of technology planning will become a very formal and expanded literature in the next ten years.

Question for Dr. Thomas and Dr. Fuller: A lot of references have been made to the quality of people, and especially of managers. What is your profile of the characteristics that identify an ideal top technical officer?

DR. THOMAS: I think it is difficult to give one profile for a top technical officer, who oversees complex operations. Certainly one of the important characteristics in technical or research management is that the person has to have a good understanding of technical issues and be able to converse with technical people about them. A second important characteristic is that really good technical leadership in the R&D function needs to be not custodial, but anticipatory, able to reach out and change things, make things happen. A third characteristic of successful technical management is the ability to

[1] See Chapters 18 and 20 for more information about this concept and its applications.

recognize what one is personally really good at, and to make sure the rest of the management team complements the chief technical officer well enough to see that the whole function is pulled together properly.

DR. FULLER: I second those comments, and add that a first-rate chief technical officer has an understanding of people and is able, therefore, to put himself in the position of other company managers in different fields and to understand what they are trying to tell him. It is rare to find somebody who has been trained in the management of things who also has an excellent understanding of people.

Part V
Exploiting Outside Resources

Introductory Remarks
Session Chairman Herbert I. Fusfeld
Director, Center for Science and Technology Policy
Graduate School of Business Administration
New York University

This session assesses outside resources that may be used for R&D. Most of the issues discussed have to do, in an important sense, with R&D productivity—that is, how a company can get the most from a given investment in R&D. Clearly, the R&D manager has a lot more at his or her disposal than internal resources.

There is growing concern with the wisest use of *all* the resources that we have in the country, and in fact, internationally. We have seen a great stress recently on university-industry cooperation. We talk a lot about government-industry cooperation. And most of the larger corporations are deeply involved with joint ventures or other forms of international collaboration.

Chapter 13
The University Connection

T.L. Tolbert
Director, External Research and Development
Monsanto Company

I have been involved with the subject of university-industry interaction since 1965. In my view, it is much more than a fad. It is, rather, a realistic, constructive approach to meeting the problems of industry, of universities, and of the nation.

In the last 15 years, industry and academe have relearned a great deal about working together constructively and collaboratively. I say relearned because there were a number of instances of effective, mutually beneficial interactions before World War II, although none on the scale that university-industry partnerships are developing now. This is due to the changing environment in which we live, mutual recognition that we can achieve things together which we cannot achieve alone and mutual understanding of what such relationships must involve to be successful.

It is generally accepted now that industry can not and should not try to be leaders in basic research in every field. This is the province of academe. Yet innovation—that is, the application and the ultimate commercialization of new science in the form of products and processes—requires that industry become cognizant of new discoveries as soon as possible.

Ideally, one would like to know of new discoveries as they are made, of new concepts as they are formulated, of new inventions as they are formalized. Clearly, this is not possible. But it is practical for specific industrial scientists and engineers, working collaboratively with their academic associates, to become aware of and gain early insights into the significance of basic observations over a broad range of technologies. They can enjoy the counsel of experts in many fields and have access to a variety of interrelated research-support systems. Research interactions with major universities, their faculties, students and supporting staff, offer to industry a window on science and a mechanism, not otherwise accessible, for transferring new knowledge. Of course, this is only the start of the innovation process, but it is a necessary start in today's scientific and engineering environment.

In turn, industrial collaborations can provide to the university financial aid, access to specialized facilities, and needed perspective in research and education. Research collaborations focusing on truly basic questions of science can be entirely consistent and supportive of the needs of both partners. Fundamental knowledge and science can be advanced, new insights gained and communicated, and students trained.

This can and must be done without altering the purpose of the university and the role it fulfills for society—its mission to educate and to conduct basic research. We in industry want to learn, and we want to learn from the very best professors. We recognize, however, that there are potential dangers in disrupting the university culture, that academic freedom must be protected, and that care must be taken to avoid excessive focusing of university efforts on commercial goals and away from fundamental studies.

Why do we in industry have this sudden need to learn? There are several factors that have become important to industry. These include:

• The time between making a discovery and having that discovery enter the commercial world is being reduced. This is particularly true in the life sciences area, which until recently has been relatively foreign to large industry.

• Technology transfer from the university also is quickening.

• More university research can now be used by industry; recombinant DNA studies are examples.

• The traditional boundaries between basic and applied research—or between university and industrial research—are blurring rapidly.

- The funding patterns for support of academic research are changing. Nondefense federal research spending has slipped some 38 percent in constant dollars since the mid-1960's, with most of this decrease occurring in the last two years.

All these factors are pushing industry and universities into a reassessment of past approaches of interaction and cooperation in science. Particularly encouraging are indications that both institutions are discovering a greater sense of community and shared interest. In short, we are finding ourselves to be logical partners for scientific innovation and technology transfer.

In the past few years, Monsanto has found a number of advantages in participating in various research collaborations. Among these is a means of adapting to competitive change. Market forces have led industry to move increasingly toward specialized products that serve basic human needs. Development of these products relies on infusion of new technology, often in fields that are wholly new. While this offers an opportunity for synergy among what have traditionally been different technologies and sciences, it also means that we have the problem of developing new expertise, assimilating new science and new scientists and transferring new technology.

Needs to Be Met

The articulation of the internal environment and the common needs that must be met for an effective university-industry partnership results in a listing of what seem to be truisms. In fact, many of these elements require special care to protect and implement.

In any agreement, whether short- or long-term, whether involving a consortium arrangement or an industrial liaison program, a research investment external to the funding organization requires both *patience* and *confidence in the value* of the basic research that will occur. It also requires *mutual trust*. From a purely business standpoint, both partners must understand *what* is expected from the contract and *how* each is to function. This is the most cost- and time-effective approach. After all, risk on both sides is higher with outside collaborators.

Another hurdle involves the whole issue of secrecy. From the university point of view, protecting the opportunity for publication and free intellectual exchange is a central issue. From industry's view, the *right to protect new discoveries* by means of patents and licensing is critical. For every dollar invested in research, hundreds more must be spent in the applications phases, and there must be a reasonable chance of protecting and recovering this investment. Both issues must be addressed.

Finally, there are the questions of *flexibility and continuity* in partnership. The first is a matter of compatibility of the two cultures; care must be taken that they be meshed, but not merged. One way to avoid disruption is to have *contracts between institutions* rather than between individuals. Although this is not always possible, we have found it to be a mechanism that works particularly well. It assures uniformity, protects individual concerns, and avoids surprises on either side.

Peer review is an important component of any such effort to ensure that the program is progressing properly. The university is assured that its efforts are of proper quality and that academic freedom continues to thrive. Industry, in turn, is provided with an objective assessment of technical progress.

Questions of *conflict of interest* and *divisiveness* also must be taken into account. An excellent approach is an agreement in which institutions, rather than individuals, profit. For example, in a recent contract between Monsanto and Washington University Medical School, royalties are divided equally among the university, the department, and the laboratories involved. Individual scientists enjoy benefits through the strengthening of their programs in their respective institutions by maintaining an equal relationship with their university and Monsanto colleagues.

Four Programs

Based on our experience at Monsanto we are convinced that the benefits of collaborating with universities can be achieved and the pitfalls avoided. The examples I offer are quite different from one another. Taken together, they indicate the range of opportunity for such collaboration.

The first program is now ancient history, but this is one of its virtues in the sense that results can be assessed from the perspective of its impact with time. In 1964, Monsanto, Washington University, and the Office of Naval Research joined in what then was called a coupling project to do fundamental research on the physics, chemistry, structural mechanics, design and processing of polymeric composites reinforced with high-modulus fibers. The program was funded by the Advanced Research Projects Agency, now DARPA, at a rate of $1 million a year for seven years.

This was a landmark contract in a variety of ways: It included both a research and education component and involved a number of graduate students, as well as senior investigators and technicians at each of the institutions. All participants enjoyed relatively free access to the laboratories and staff of the two sister institutions, with students conducting research both at Washington University and at Monsanto. A total of 28 degrees resulted from the project, and nearly 100 publications and 30 patents were generated over its life.

Of particular interest and satisfaction to me is that six clearly identifiable and successful commercial innovations ensued. While none was generated by the project per se, its contributions to their development are clearly traceable. One of these, a reinforcing material called Santoweb, is produced by Monsanto. Basic understanding of the chemistry and interfacial character of reinforcement in another recently introduced Monsanto product, a new injection moldable nylon called Nyrim, also was advanced by the DARPA-funded studies. The remaining innovations resulted from subsequent work of project "graduates," each with a different company now, who continued their work in fiber and particulate reinforced composites after leaving the university.

This project was Monsanto's first experience in large-scale, collaborative interaction with academe. We view it as a very favorable, constructive experience in many ways. It was the genesis of the extensive program in university collaboration that we now enjoy, even though most of our present programs are biologically, rather than engineering and materials, oriented—notably our programs at Harvard, Rockefeller, and Washington Universities.

It was in the DARPA-funded project that we began to learn how some of the key issues in working together can be resolved to the mutual good of each partner. We gained confidence that the tenets of academic freedom can be preserved while meeting proprietary concerns. Most important, we gained confidence in the value of fundamental research done externally and became comfortable working with our academic colleagues in an atmosphere of mutual support and trust.

A second, quite different program, in which Monsanto is participating involves support of research by promising junior faculty members working in the forefront of quite fundamental areas of technology. The program itself is still something of an experiment and so is relatively small, although we are quite pleased with the progress so far.

A revolving fund administered by a faculty committee has been established at MIT to support three concurrent programs, chosen from forty proposals, in the physical and biological sciences for periods of two to three years each. Monsanto participation focuses on active collaboration with the university investigators to decide on the directions the programs will take.

Advantages to Monsanto are the development of what we hope will be meaningful long-term relationships with a variety of young, high-quality scientists at the university, and, of course, licensing opportunities in areas where we are not now working in depth. Advantages to the faculty participants are funding for their early research and generation of publishable results, which can serve as a basis for future funding by industry (including Monsanto) or by government.

The next example of university-industry interaction is one in which we are participating with 38 other companies and about 140 universities. It is conducted under the aegis of the Council of Chemical Research (CCR). This is a voluntary organization that grew out of a meeting four years ago of chemical industry and university leaders to discuss the need for closer cooperation and to establish a permanent body to explore what can be done to institute appropriate programs. The Council has four objectives: to promote mutual understanding and cooperation between academe and industry; to work toward improving the national climate for creativity and innovation; to promote the education of highly qualified science and engineering professionals to meet the needs of academe, government and industry; to provide colleges and universities with new, significant and continuing sources of funding for basic research of potential value to industry.

The CCR has a number of active committees of rotating membership from industry and the universities to explore ways of promoting interaction. These include such things as development of model contracts, guidelines for joint research programs or sponsored research, and several pilot programs in which individual departments and a member industry test alternative approaches to collaboration.

Another aspect of the CCR program is a central fund used to encourage and strengthen education and research in chemistry and chemical engineering. The fund is provided through voluntary donations, according to a formula reflecting the number of chemical and chemical engineering graduates employed by the member companies. The fund is then distributed to university departments based on their production of Ph.D's.

CCR undoubtedly will change with time. The important thing is that it has become a reality. It is growing and it is working. We in Monsanto feel that we have gotten some definable benefit from our participation. In my view, CCR and similar programs, such as those sponsored by the American Electrical Association and Semiconductor Industries Association, are important approaches to gaining closer cooperation and mutual support between industry and education.

My last example—one that does not require much investment—is an informal industry-sponsored program for technology transfer chaired by Aladdin Industries. About two years ago, Mr. A.L. Frye, senior vice president for research at Aladdin, and executives from Monsanto and three other companies decided that more information was needed on the expertise available and on new discoveries at major U.S. research universities. They began an experiment that continues to expand and bear fruit. The approach is simple. It involves meetings, at industry expense, with representatives of universities and government laboratories in different parts of the country. The meetings, held every two months, last for a day and a half. We listen to brief presentations by university representatives and then hold one-on-one discussions to pursue topics of particular interest to a given industry. It is left to the individual industrial members to follow up as appropriate.

Our industry group, now numbering 25, is selected to minimize competitive conflict among the members. It represents both large and small firms. Among the members are such varied companies as Aladdin Industries, Monsanto, Bendix, Ferro Corporation, Amway Corporation, S.D. Johnson, International Minerals and Chemical Corporation, and A.E. Staley Manufacturing Company. University and government participants now number over 100 in all parts of the country.

The most important news is that this informal arrangement works and most of us have had some hits. This means technology has been gained for industry and a significantly higher level of support achieved for participating universities.

Our industry group is about as large as it can get to maintain good contact during the meetings. But there is no reason why others cannot initiate a similar program designed to meet the needs of their own companies and industries.

These four very different approaches to collaborating with academe are by no means the only ones that will work. They may, however, suggest ideas for programs that will fit the particular interests of other companies and industries.

Chapter 14
Licensing—Technology Transfer for Profit

Mary L. Good
Vice President-Director of Research
UOP, Inc.—One of the Signal Companies

The concept of licensing technology for the economic enhancement of the portfolios of licensee and licensor is certainly not new. It has been a major contributor to the diversification of our technologically driven industries and it has played a significant role in the growth of technology in the developing countries. Thus, it is not surprising that a significant literature has developed which addresses the various issues of licensing.[1] I want to focus on the general principles associated with satisfactory licensing and an explanation of the current status of licensing potential within the United States.

A technology licensing package normally serves to transfer the use of patents, trademarks or other proprietary technology from the technology developer to the technology user.[2] The package may also contain technical and managerial assistance to the licensee. For such packages to be successful they must provide mutual satisfaction and profit for licensee and licensor. As Dr. Willard Marcy of Research Corporation has said: "Licensing technology mut be a friendly act between two willing partners."[3] The responsibility of each partner has

been clearly delineated by C.J. Giuliani, former president of the Process Division of UOP, Inc., who wrote, in 1975, that there must be a "sense of mutual trust and dependence upon the licensor to come forward and deliver to the expectations of the licensee." Understanding these basic requirements for successful licensing leads one to assess the appropriate role of licensing in comparison with other methods of technology acquisitions in various business environments.

Technology acquisition can occur by internal development, the purchase of fully developed technology, or licensing. Each method has pros and cons, and appropriate business strategy depends on the individual situation.

The filing of patent applications is the normal route chosen for basic science and fundamental technology discoveries and developments. Patents provide several advantages including: exclusive business protection of new ideas, defense against competitors, availability of new and/or improved technology for income generation from licensing and royalties, and the enhancement of present "know-how" for future business development.[4] In-house patent positions also provide a competitive negotiating position for external technology acquisition, and they generate an in-house awareness of technology availability since less than 1 percent of the patent information is published elsewhere.

Sources

It is useful to review the various sources of patents, intellectual property and new technology. The sources are diverse and their motivations for intellectual property

[1]A complete list of definitive references on licensing is beyond the scope of this paper, but general and informative sources include the following:
   a. A. Biaco and L. Gastwirt, *Turning Research and Development Into Profits.* New York: Amacom, a Division of American Management Association, 1979; and
   b. Farok J. Contractor, *International Technology Licensing: Compensation, Costs, and Negotiations.* Lexington, MA: D.C. Heath, 1982.

[2]Farok J. Contractor, "The Composition of Licensing Fees and Arrangements as a Function of Economic Development of Technology Recipient Nations." *Journal of International Business Studies,* Winter, 1980, p. 47.

[3]Willard Marcy, "Acquiring and Selling Technology—Licensing Do's and Don'ts." *Research Management,* May, 1979, p. 18.

[4]George Stuart, "Technology Transfer—Patents and Licenses." *Planned Innovation,* January-February, 1980, p. 19.

States. They are, however, also very much aware of outside licensing opportunities, as indicated by the fact that 81 percent license from outside the United States, 80 percent license from individuals, 40 percent license from universities or their faculties, and 20 percent license from government-owned inventions.[6] These statistics indicate that the major sources of new technology reside in that fraction of the industrial sector that performs in-house R&D, and that the larger part of the licensing which takes place is among organizations in this category. Most of these organizations, however, do not place a heavy emphasis on external licensing, and there are few examples of companies whose major income is derived from licensing fees and royalties. Thus, if increased technology transfer is to occur through licensing, it is important to sensitize both potential licensees and licensors to the additional business opportunities that exist through this mechanism.

Fertile Fields

Opportunities for licensing occur in many areas, but a few fields are especially fertile. Process licenses are an example. It can be particularly profitable for both licensee and licensor when a process that produces a unique product, decreases product costs, improves product quality, or lends itself to a "first-to-market" joint venture can be licensed. Manufacturers of volume product lines can take special advantage of outside technology to enhance their product properties, increase product volume, improve production efficiency, improve available accessories, improve packaging, and/or enhance service. Such techniques can lengthen product life cycles and ensure profitability beyond that possible with the original product technology.[7] Another profitable concept is that of "niche" licensing; here a company with extensive capital invested in manufacturing equipment can license outside technology to make a new product that uses existing manufacturing capability or that allows the extension of a current product line to new but related areas. These advantages of outside technology are well understood by many manufacturing organizations that lack R&D resources to develop the required technology in-house. To be successful at retrieving appropriate technology at the right time, however, such organizations need to develop "technology awareness" in their staffs, and they must designate some office or group as the technology development leader charged with the responsibility of determining where their product line

development are quite varied. The major sources include: (1) individual, unaffiliated inventors, (2) small incorporated laboratories, (3) nonprofit research institutes, (4) universities, (5) government units, and (6) other industrial entities.[5]

Examples of major contributions emanate from each of these sources, but the frequency of such occurrences is very different for each source. Independent inventors have been the source of a number of "next generation" technologies but the majority of new process, new product, and improved product or process technology has come from R&D efforts of industrial organizations. For example, of the 1,162,000 U.S. patents presently in force, 75 percent are owned by corporations, 23 percent by individuals, and 2 percent by government and universities. Members of the Industrial Research Institute, an organization of companies that have significant corporate R&D activity, presently carry out 84 percent of the industrially funded research in the United

[5]Murray Senkus, "Acquiring and Selling Technology—Licensing Sources and Resources." *Research Management*, May, 1979, p. 22.

[6]"Acquiring and Marketing Technology—Industrial Research Institute Position Statement on Licensing of Technology." *Research Management*, May, 1979, p. 32.

[7]Robert A. Linn, "The When and Why of Licensed Technology." *Research Management*, July, 1981, p. 21.

needs help and how to acquire that help. In addition, they must be prepared technically to exploit the acquired technology in a timely and efficient manner.

From the viewpoint of possible licensors, the potential for increased revenues from outside licensing is just beginning to be realized by many organizations that do significant in-house R&D in support of their present businesses. These organizations make up the bulk of R&D producers and their main emphasis is on improving and expanding their business lines. In general, they do not focus on opportunities for licensing their technology, since part of their R&D effort is to meet and overcome competition. These groups are beginning to recognize, however, that they may have a source of added revenue in their "off-line" inventions, those discoveries that are not competitive with their main business areas but that have been reported by their employees during their work on company-oriented projects. These inventions are usually related to company operations, but may not represent an "in-house" advantage. Usually in these circumstances, patent applications are not made until an initial market survey has indicated a profitability potential after all patent costs are recovered. Sometimes patents may be pursued to gain experience or to get visibility in the marketplace, to enhance current business or the ability to market other technology. How extensive and useful this activity can be depends on the particular case, but the potential for transferring valuable technology may be quite great. This area needs further study and exploration.

Keys to Licensor Success

For those few companies that aggressively develop new technology for licensing, the keys to licensor success can best be summed up by paraphrasing the remarks of Mr. C.J. Giuliani, former president of the UOP Process Division. His seven keys to success are:

(1) Technical superiority (technical personnel; assessment of overall technology base)

(2) Singlemindedness of purpose (some definable entity should be established with licensing as its primary goal)

(3) Integrated organization with team approach

(4) "One-stop" shopping (technology coverage; services for licensee)

(5) Ability to show high profitability for licensee

(6) Well-conceived, "agreement" package mutually advantageous (performance guarantees; engineering agreements; service agreements)

(7) Appropriate and "personalized" relationship between licensee and licensor.

This approach to technology developed for licensing requires an unusual dedication to ongoing R&D

programs and a highly motivated and interacting staff who have the confidence to bring new developments from the laboratory to the pilot plants and, finally, to the marketplace quickly. But many of the concepts are applicable to the occasional licensor that has technology of value but no in-house plans for its exploitation.

Technology and the National Strategic Plan

So far we have looked at what constitutes licensing and how both potential licensee and licensor can benefit. The next question concerns the role technology development and transfer plays, or should play, in our national strategic plan. One way of evaluating past performance is to examine our national balance of payments. A comparison of the trade balance for R&D-intensive industries with that of non-R&D-intensive activities indicates that, between 1972 and 1980, the overall balance *rose* from $11 billion to $52.5 billion for R&D-intensive trading and *dropped* from -$16 billion to -$33.5 billion for non-R&D-intensive trade.[8] The performance of R&D-intensive products over the past few years is also informative, as shown in the tabulation below:

U.S. Trade Balance for R&D Intensive Products
(in billions of dollars)

Country or Region	Year		
	1972	1978	1980
Japan	$ + 3.0	$ + 10.0	$ + 14.5
Western Europe	-.971	- 5.7	- 3.6
Developing Countries	+ 5.3	+ 17.9	+ 29.8

Source: U.S. Department of Commerce, Domestic and International Business Administration, *Overseas Business Reports,* various dates.

Another measure of the value of R&D-intensive activities is shown in the comparison of the balance of payments for royalties and fees from international licensing.

Balance of Payments for Royalties and Licensing Fees
(in billions of dollars)

Country or Region	Year		
	1972	1978	1981
Western Europe	$0.938	$2.2	$2.7
Japan	0.335	0.390	0.812
Developing Countries	0.530	0.967	1.85

Source: Meryl L. Kroner, "U.S. International Transactions in Royalties and Fees." *Survey of Current Business,* 1980, Vol. 64, p. 34, and unpublished data from the U.S. Department of Commerce.

[8]U.S. Department of Commerce, Domestic and International *Business Administration, Overseas Business Reports.* August, 1967; April, 1972; April, 1977; August, 1979; July, 1980; November, 1981.

The definitions used to develop these figures were: Royalties are payments for the use of copyrights or trademarks, and licensing fees are charges for the use of a patent or industrial process. These statistics are impressive in that they clearly indicate the U.S. dependence on R&D-intensive products in international trade. It is particularly striking that our balance in intellectual property is significant and growing even with Japan. Thus an important issue is: Are we prepared to continue this trade advantage in R&D-intensive industries? The question is particularly relevant if we look at some data on our knowledge base, and how well we are exploiting that base in the production of patents.

The U.S. contribution to the scientific literature in the crucial fields of science seems to be holding its own, as indicated by the following figures:

Proportion of World Literature by U.S. Authors

	Percent of Total			
Field	1973	1977	1979	1980
Biomedicine	39	39	40	40
Biology	46	42	43	42
Chemistry	23	22	21	21
Physics	33	30	30	30
Engineering and Technology	42	40	41	38
Mathematics	48	41	40	40

Source: National Science Foundation unpublished data compiled by Computer Horizons, Inc.

Except for mathematics, the relative decline of U.S. scientific literature over this period has been small, although the four percentage point decline in engineering and technology may be especially significant because of the special relationship between engineering and technology and communication. In any event, the scientific literature base must be used to produce products or processes of value. The first step is the conversion of the fundamental science into potentially commercial ideas or patents. Chart 1 indicates a significant decline in U.S. patents granted to U.S. inventors from 1971 to 1980. Time will tell if the 1980-1981 increase marks a new trend. Note that the scale of the figure is in numbers of patents, not percent of total. For example, the total U.S. patents awarded to U.S. inventors fell from a high of 56,011 in 1971 to a low of 30,079 in 1979 and returned to 39,224 in 1981. (The 1979 data are incomplete because the Patent and Trademark Office did not have enough money that year to print all approved patents.) This overall decline in U.S. patent productivity is also shown in Chart 2, where patents granted to U.S. inventors by selected countries are in-

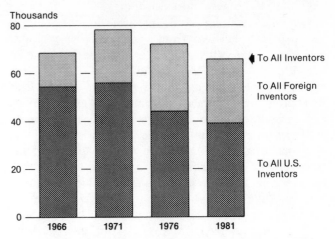

Chart 1
U.S. Patents Granted to Domestic and Foreign Inventors

Source: Office, Technology Assessment and Forecast, U.S. Patent and Trademark Office. "Indicators of Patent Output of U.S. Industry, 1963-1981," June, 1982.

dicated. Here there is yet no evidence of an upturn, although 1981 and 1982 figures are not available.

These data indicate to me that it is in the country's best interests to stimulate the development of intellectual property by whatever means we have. Some recent legal cases may abode well for the further patent protection of new intellectual ideas in the computer field and the promising field of biotechnology. In Diamond v. Chakrabarty, the Supreme Court [44 of U.S. 303 (1980)] clearly ruled that manmade organisms are patentable, and the ruling in Diamond v. Diehr [450 U.S. 175 (1981)] has made it possible to patent appropriate process-related software. The early acceptance and licensing of the Stanford University DNA process patent are also indications of the value of such seminal ideas.

Let me conclude with these observations:

(1) Creation of intellectual property is a production process that enhances the country's technological position.

(2) The utilization of U.S.-developed intellectual property has significant economic advantages both in domestic and foreign markets.

(3) The encouragement of mutually beneficial licensing is in the best interests of our industrial and national competitiveness.

(4) Ways should be explored to increase innovation and technology development by improving the business climate for R&D-intensive companies, by evaluating government regulations which hinder innovative technology, and by reviewing tax incentives to make R&D a more attractive corporate activity.

Chart 2

Patents Granted to U.S. Inventors by Selected Foreign Countries

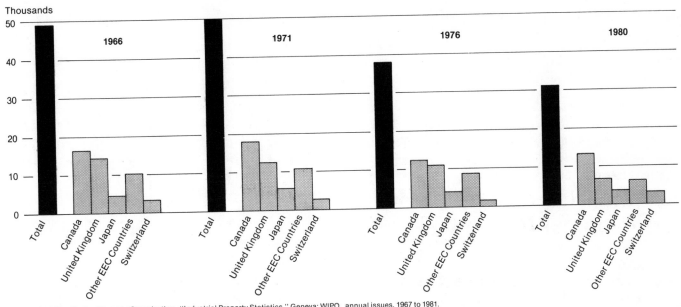

Source: World Intellectual Property Organization. "Industrial Property Statistics," Geneva: WIPO, annual issues, 1967 to 1981.

Chapter 15
Capitalizing on Foreign Research and Development

Dr. Leon C. Greene
Vice President, New Compound Evaluation &
    Licensing
Smith Kline & French Laboratories

Capitalizing on foreign research and development is not a new notion. I have been involved in the research and development of compounds worldwide for 25 years. But I am following a tradition established long before I became a worldwide project director.

First, a bit of history. Smith Kline and French Laboratories, if not the first to explore opportunities abroad, was clearly one of the first pharmaceutical firms to do so. In the early 1950's, Francis Boyer, who was then president of Smith Kline and French Laboratories, was pioneering the practice of searching foreign markets for information useful to his firm. He journeyed to Latin America, winning the citizens there with his knowledge of Spanish and his easy adjustment to their way of life.

He conquered the French with the same qualities—his appreciation of their culture, his love of their country, his knowledge of their history, and his ability to speak their language fluently. His motivation for the trip to France was part hunch and part scientific curiosity. He was not satisfied to talk just with the company people, but visited the hospital wards where the medicines were in use. On one occasion, he took note of what were perceived by the Europeans to be side effects of a particular antihistamine and antiemetic.

His acute observation of the important behavioral effects of this compound resulted in a cooperative venture between the French company and his—and in SK&F's marketing of the phenothiazines as major tranquilizers. This series of events virtually revolutionized care of the mentally ill worldwide. What Boyer found, and I'll use his words, was that "European pharmaceutical houses also recognized the need for well-developed cooperation with academic medicine." Boyer saw that these firms had succeeded in building contacts with academic institutions as he wanted to do. And he observed that it was not easy for a foreign concern to place its own drugs on the U.S. market.

Boyer certainly had hit on a concept that was ready for cultivating. Today, SmithKline Beckman, as well as dozens of other U.S. pharmaceutical companies, are pursuing the course he pioneered. Also, there are new pressures on investigative scientists and those responsible for the management of research and development on a worldwide basis. Pharmaceutical researchers today must deal with rapid growth of knowledge in their own and other scientific disciplines, but with the accelerated pace with which we do business as well. They must also learn to accommodate their work to two other issues: (1) sharply rising costs, and (2) shrinking periods of patent protection. More about these two points later.

Long-Distance Management

Managing R&D projects on a global level carries with it many complexities. I would like to offer some insight into four facets of worldwide R&D—the management of the long-distance relationships; the complexities of actual clinical studies; satisfaction of both domestic and foreign regulatory requirements; and the impact of worldwide R&D on the patent area. Just as in managing a domestic clinical study, working with a worldwide study involves all major areas of drug development—pharmaceutical chemistry, pharmacology and clinical studies, to name a few. But that is where the similarities end. If a compound originated in another country, there are scientific as well as semipolitical implications for the U.S. developer and marketer. One must keep the originating company informed of the progress. In effect, one is working with its "family jewels," and must not lose sight of its right to full information.

That is why frequent communication is imperative. Memos and telephone calls are certainly vital. But the best way of communicating is in person—face-to-face, at least four times a year—admittedly an expensive habit. I have found, however, that even *more* frequent face-to-face meetings result in stronger, ongoing relationships—relationships that will continue to be rewarding and profitable. Such intensive interaction is always worth the money. For example, the exchange of information with medical directors relating to clinical trials of past accomplishments, current work, and future plans results in a cross-fertilization of ideas, as well as adding new worldwide dimensions to a project. It is important that these meetings be held in different parts of the world so that the various organizations feel they are a key part and have a key responsibility to the developing programs. At the same time, this affords the worldwide project director an opportunity to encounter and deal with cultural differences and, from time to time, to meet with regulatory organizations in that country. More concerning the regulatory scene later.

Frequent meetings are a key to overcoming one particular obstacle faced when managing a long-distance project. That obstacle is the NIH syndrome—not the National Institutes of Health, but the "not-invented-here" syndrome. One can have all the best intentions, planning thoroughly to avoid duplication of effort, and covering all the regulatory bases. But if the scientists and clinicians in one's own country are not behind the project, or are not "champions" of it, it will not progress. They have to come to believe in the work, even though it may not be their "brainchild." Once there is a "champion" for such a project, though, the NIH syndrome disappears.

There is also the reverse problem—the feeling in the foreign cooperating firm that it has become a "junior partner." Frequent meetings on foreign turf can dispel the feeling that the project revolves around the United States, and can promote an appreciation of the data from a worldwide point of view.

Clinical Trials

I have touched on a few key issues of long-distance management—building relationships, cementing loyalties, maintaining communication. But these are not ends in themselves. They fuel the primary effort, the clinical trial. We are talking about taking compounds that have been developed either here or abroad and testing them on humans for efficacy and safety world-wide. These studies are necessary steps in product development. Obviously, it is important that they be thorough.

When one is responsible for the development of a new pharmaceutical on a worldwide basis, it is not enough to have the protocols and clinical procedures translated into foreign languages. Of course, the meaning of every word must be clearly understood. But, even more important, the concepts and objectives must be understood, appreciated and accepted by the medical communities in participating countries. Here are examples of how differences in points of view and different medical standards can affect a study.

When we were developing the anti-ulcer drug, "Tagamet," we in the United States took for granted that we were aiming for maximum gastric-acid inhibition. But we soon discovered that view was not shared by our counterparts in other countries. At a meeting in London of 60 gastroenterologists from all over the world, the physicians literally split into camps based on what constituted adequate inhibition for healing an ulcer.

Sound confusing? It can be very much so. But we dare not let the confusion get the better of us. Clinical studies do not stop for the holidays, as I found out one Christmas Eve. We were testing a flu vaccine on married couples in Australia. We vaccinated the husbands. But the wives started coming down with flu. It looked as if there had been some shedding of the virus—something we did not want to happen. We finally did cultures on the wives' strain of flu and found that it was a new strain of virus—not the same strain as our vaccination.

At the very same time, we had the identical situation in an orphanage in Boston, where we were testing a vaccine for German measles. The head of the orphanage was calling us, accusing us of spreading the disease among the children. Again, we eventually determined that the orphans were contracting another viral infection with some of the same symptoms.

These things happen and we learn to deal with them. But it takes some doing for a worldwide project director sitting in Philadelphia on Christmas Eve confronting apparent snafus in Australia and Boston that could seriously mar two clinical studies and potential products.

Government Regulations

Government regulations have been a fact of life for pharmaceutical concerns for as long as most of us can remember. To get approval for a new product, we have to satisfy the U.S. Food and Drug Administration, as well as many foreign regulatory agencies. Here at home, the FDA requires truly controlled studies to support the efficacy and safety claims of any compound. Those data are required whether the study was performed here or abroad, and the rules are rigid and closely monitored.

Most often, that means studies of the type known as

"double blind." That means neither the patients nor the investigators know who received the investigated drug and who received the control substance until the study is complete and the code is broken. But, some foreign medical communities, where part of the study may be taking place, are not accustomed to such rigid requirements. In those cases, the foreign clinicians may generate uncontrolled data. This can present complications in terms of U.S. assessment and evaluation. It can even create a misleading picture of adverse effects mistakenly attributed to the compound. Such studies may be acceptable by regulatory agencies in some countries, but they create complications on the regulatory scene here in the United States.

There are also differences from country to country about what constitutes evidence of efficacy. As evidence for efficacy, well-controlled, scientific data are a must in the United States. In some European countries, however, the opinion of an expert as to the drug's effects is often accepted as evidence without supporting documentation. The FDA wants hard, indisputable data on both safety *and* efficacy. But do not let me mislead you into thinking that all foreign regulatory agencies are less demanding than the FDA. Australia, Germany, Japan and the United Kingdom, along with the United States and Canada, continue to have the most demanding regulatory agencies for the approval of new pharmaceuticals.

It is important for anyone responsible for a worldwide research and development project to understand and appreciate the requirements for the approval of new drugs on a worldwide basis. I find that the best way to work with foreign agencies is directly—in France, Germany, Italy, or any nation. Foreign governments welcome discussions with people from the U.S. pharmaceutical industry. These officials are delighted to talk to someone who has a thorough familiarity with the U.S. regulatory scene. What one must accept is that at least 50 percent of such meetings consists of describing one's own relationship with the U.S. Food and Drug Administration.

As far as changes in foreign bureaucracies are concerned, we have a lot of practice in coping with that situation. Consider that it can take six to ten years to develop a new compound in preparation for marketing. Here in the United States we could have two or three changes in FDA management by the time a drug makes it through the approval process. Disagreements come and go as administrations do likewise. It is something we are used to dealing with. On the brighter side of that issue, France is an example of a country in which the old guard opinion makers are being replaced by "young Turks." That is not all bad. Many of the younger people have been trained in the science of the 1970's and 1980's. They truly do understand what a controlled clinical trial is. And they have an appreciation for statistical analysis as against the "expert opinion" mode which was mentioned earlier. This is often because many of these people have been trained abroad—frequently in the United States.

Patents

Of course, all these issues lead to the last chapter in any R&D project, the drug's patent. It must be understood that the ethical pharmaceutical industry is a patent-based industry. By that, I mean that exclusivity in the marketplace, afforded by effective patent protection, is the cornerstone of the industry, has made it what it is, and is necessary for its continued existence. It is no wonder then, that strong, effective and respected worldwide patents and patent systems are so vital. It is well recognized that patents become an eroding asset of most pharmaceutical companies all too quickly. In fact, the average term of patent protection actually afforded the pharmaceutical industry in the United States is approximately only eight to nine years of a seventeen-year patent. Legislation has been proposed and is needed which would restore the patent terms of new compounds for the length of time lost due to regulatory approval processes.

As an industry, we continue to attempt to extend the patent life on new compounds. We file them as broadly and as extensively as possible to protect corporate assets. That means we file for patents in every country that recognizes them. And sometimes we synthesize and patent hundreds of related chemical compounds to protect just one product. With six to ten years needed for development of a new therapeutic agent, and the $50-to-$100 million price tag on that research and development, trying to extend the patent and the payback on that product is an understandable effort. And since at best two out of ten agents taken into development actually see any success, the need for this extensive patenting effort becomes even more clear.

The concepts Francis Boyer pioneered 30 years ago are still valid—perhaps more so today. In his time, the practice of capitalizing on foreign R&D efforts grew slowly. Today it is accelerating for many reasons. Among the factors that are making such overseas relationships easier and more fruitful are:

(1) The frequency and ease of travel around the world;
(2) The increase in the number of scientific meetings;
(3) The increase in the number of Europeans who study in the United States;
(4) The increasing sophistication of other countries in their R&D technology.

By having an agreement with a foreign company or academic institution, we are in a position to blend our R&D activities and theirs. If a single investigative compound fails—and many do—at least we have created a continuing relationship that may well be productive later. The significant risks and costs of experimentation, as well as the potential profits, can be shared and spread more broadly. International cooperation among pharmaceutical firms is clearly with us and is a wave of the future. And U.S. pharmaceutical company management would be well advised to ride that wave through the 1980's and beyond.

Chapter 16
Joint Research Ventures

Peter F. McCloskey
President
Electronic Industries Association

Perhaps no other sector of our economy is viewed with such high expectation as research and development—and not without cause. It has truly been the fuel that has driven our mighty economic engine during the post-World War II period. And yet there is a sense of apprehension in the air as we face the challenges of international competition in the final years of this century; a fuller realization that we do not have a corner on the market of brains and that a large part of our post-World War II success was that our industrial might had not been damaged by the war but was, in fact, enhanced. We were poised and ready and, as a nation, took advantage of it. And we grew complacent, mistaking the temporary advantage for the imagined natural superiority of the United States in the area of high technology.

There can be no mistake about it: Our complacency has been shaken. Our advantages have turned into disadvantages, and we are now grappling with new realities. The industrial plant of our principal international competitors—Japan and Germany—has been rebuilt, or perhaps more properly, built anew. They did not merely repair their old plant and equipment; rather, they embraced the latest technology and in so doing were able in many cases to leapfrog past our older plant. They were the best customers for the U.S. machine tool industry. They looked to us for technology—and they found it. Through licensing arrangements, technology was transferred to give them a leg up on rebuilding their economies.

Meanwhile, the size of our domestic market made it unnecessary for the medium-sized U.S. firm to seek exports to support its growth. This was not so for our trading partners. They absolutely needed export markets to grow, and their sights were set firmly on the largest export market—the United States. In the last five years

many U.S. companies have awakened to the realization that although they are not in the export marketplace (as they should be), they are nonetheless in the international marketplace. Increasingly, domestic U.S. companies are losing market share in the United States to nondomestic producers. The miracles of communication and transportation—the satellite and the jumbo jet—have shrunk the world marketplace so that it is available to all who want to "go for it." And particularly appealing is the U.S. market—because it is the most open market, with relatively few non-tariff barriers, and a population drawn from all parts of the globe, whose citizens are more willing to buy the best product at the best price than any other people on earth.

Our Strengths and Vulnerabilities

It is certainly not a time to despair, but it is time to turn our advantages back into real advantages—indeed, to leverage them as best we can to ensure our role as the world leader in technology. In my opinion, there is no question that our centers of scientific learning are unquestionably the best. We have more qualified students than ever attending these institutions, and the whole world knows it. Thus, we are also attracting the best from around the world. A few statistics are, perhaps, more ominous in this context. In 1980, almost 50 percent of all U.S. engineering doctoral degrees were awarded to foreign nationals, compared to 25 percent a decade earlier. Our commitment to research and development on an absolute scale also leads the world—but the trends are equally ominous. R&D has declined over the last 20 years from 3 percent of U.S. GNP to approximately 2.2 percent. At the same time, the Japanese and Germans have increased R&D as a portion of GNP from 1.5

percent and 1.6 percent, to 1.9 percent and 2.3 percent, respectively, while the U.S. share of government-financed R&D has declined from 2 percent to 1.2 percent during that interval. Furthermore, theirs was always focused much more on commercially realizable projects. Particularly in Japan, R&D is increasingly rationalized or, to be more accurate, targeted. That is to say that, under Public Law 84, the Japanese Government plays a role in rationalizing industry; discouraging non-competitive companies and cartelizing the remainder; organizing joint research ventures; sharing the technology among the various participants; using administrative guidance to discourage foreign competition; providing funds for the research; and working in a host of other ways to support, nurture and develop Japanese industry.

On the other hand, we basically have had a governmental "hands off" philosophy, which traditionally has served us well. Except for space and defense-related research, the government has played little role in guiding our industrial sector. And, unfortunately in my view, the transfer of technology from the sectors the government has been involved in to the commercial sector has been slow, inhibited in part by the national-security label most of it bears.

The Promise and the Barriers

There are many things that we can do to ensure our technical vitality in the future, but perhaps none would be so salient and come with less cost than facilitating joint research. Our rugged individualism, combined with uncertainty over the application of our antitrust laws, has inhibited the use of joint research as a weapon in the industrial arsenal of the United States; and yet, properly applied, it could be the most effective. In the past, when a common need was felt—whether it was a volunteer fire department or raising a barn—we have been able to work together. Now another common need has arisen. We must continue to fund our engine of progress, or horn of plenty, and we must do so more aggressively than ever if we are not to lose our natural advantages.

The first need is for legislative clarification and simplification of antitrust law as it relates to joint research. Once that is accomplished, what is needed is the will to use the tool made available. Happily, there is interest in doing precisely that. William Baxter, the Assistant Attorney General for antitrust, is very open in the area of joint research, provided that the percentage of market share of those participating in the joint research venture does not reach a certain threshold, which may vary by industry sector. In his opinion, that is about 25 percent in the electronics area. He feels there ought to be competitive joint research ventures. But he argues that if we were to put all of our eggs into one basket, we would not have competitive research ventures. Indeed we would, in effect, limit the amount of research done.

That has happened in the past. Take as an example the time when the auto industry jointly licensed all of the technology for pollution control. An antitrust suit was brought in which the claim was made that no individual company had an incentive to develop individually catalytic converters and the like, because it had to share that technology with all the other companies, and thus would not have a market advantage. As a result, the industry abandoned joint licensing.

On the legislative front, a number of proposals have been floated. These range from providing complete immunity from civil and criminal antitrust statutes for joint research ventures that either meet Justice Department guidelines and go through a business review procedure, or meet guidelines to be established by legislation. Currently there are two different bills in both the House and the Senate plus an Administration proposal for single-damage (as against treble-damage) liability, but without guidelines for overt activity. In addition, Senators Glenn, Kennedy and Laxault have yet to reintroduce the bill for complete immunity they introduced in the last Congress. While it might be optimistic to expect passage of legislation this year, many are working toward that goal.

Perhaps the more important question is: Will industry use the tool? As I mentioned earlier, joint research by companies (not jointly sponsored research conducted by universities) has been very rare. Yet effectively planned joint research obviously has some tremendous advantages. It can certainly leverage the amount of research that is being done. It can eliminate redundant or needlessly duplicative competitive research. It can enlarge the scope of research, particularly basic research. Less than 5 percent of the total research and development done by industry is basic research. Part of that problem is the cost and the unknown payoff. With joint research ventures, more basic research can be afforded.

That seems to be changing. MCC—the Microelectronics & Computer Technology Corporation—is an example. This is a joint venture of ten major electronic and computer companies founded a few months ago. Its members include Control Data, Honeywell, Sperry, RCA, Motorola, Digital Equipment, Harris, NCR, National Semiconductor Corporation, and Advanced Micro Devices. Its organization has been sanctioned by a clearance letter from William Baxter, although he has reserved the right to determine whether MCC's future activities are pro-competitive or anticompetitive. According to press reports on January 25, 1983, initial efforts will be focused on advanced computer architecture, component packaging, software productivity, and computer-aided design and manufacturing.

But MCC was called into question two days later when

the chief executives of these companies received a letter from a prominent attorney, challenging the legality of the venture and exhorting the companies involved to abandon it and to rely exclusively on individual efforts. To those who have said that our antitrust laws are flexible enough already, and that the review procedure in the Department of Justice is adequate, let me quote this attorney's words: "The reported 'clearance' letter from the Antitrust Division of the Department of Justice is not remarkable. Even a student of the antitrust laws knows that the present Antitrust Division, under the aegis of Mr. William Baxter, has abdicated its historical responsibility to enforce the law—a 'clearance' letter from the Antitrust Division is not an authorized grant of immunity from private antitrust enforcement. Neither the courts, the law, nor private parties are the least bit bound by Mr. Baxter's philosophy of what the antitrust laws should say or how they should be interpreted."

Perhaps this attorney will find a client to bring an action against MCC. In any event, neither MCC nor other joint ventures are likely to go far until the antitrust issue is clarified.

I believe that it is absurd to deny ourselves the benefits of joint research because of the uncertainty surrounding these laws. I hope there will be corporate support for legislation to provide the degree of certainty of application necessary to allow U.S. companies to leverage their research for the benefit of everyone.

Chapter 17
Questions and Answers

Question for Dr. Tolbert: If a company has tens of thousands of dollars instead of tens of millions of dollars invested in university relations, what kind of association or relationship is likely to be the most productive?

DR. TOLBERT: A technology-transfer approach such as that organized by Aladdin Industries. It is cheap and offers a very broad menu of options with emphasis on defined results..

Question for Dr. Tolbert: Please identify the criteria you use to assess the value to Monsanto of specific interactions—for example, between Monsanto and Harvard.

DR. TOLBERT: If a new program is being considered, it has to be in some way complementary or supplementary to existing research or a defined research interest, which means looking at strategic plans. If the program is already in progress and one wants to know whether it is fruitful, there is no good measure except time. But one should begin to see pertinent information within three years.

Question for Dr. Tolbert: About the patent issue: Do you always assign the rights to the university? Does it depend on the market position of the company? Does it depend on whether Monsanto funds everything in contract form, as against long-term grants? How do you divide the assignment of patent rights?

DR. TOLBERT: Each case is considered independently. By and large, we are pretty liberal. If project goals are shorter-term, fairly basic or explanatory in nature, rights are unrestricted, since it is the insight or knowledge we want. If more money is involved, then the least we want is the right to use the information. And if still more money is involved, we may well want a first option on an exclusive patent. In each case, we are working with a different culture, a different university, and agreements must fit with that institution's own policies.

Question for Dr. Tolbert: How do you justify your membership in the Chemical Council for Research? What value do you get out of it?

DR. TOLBERT: We've already seen improved relevance in terms of what the departments we are interacting with consider important. That does not mean that their work has applications—oriented or focused on commercial issues, but that fundamental questions are asked in a different way. We have felt that we have had better access to students and have been able to identify a higher quality of student. We have had one instance of synergy.

Question for Dr. Good: How do you decide between licensing and development by joint venture?

DR. GOOD: One part of our Process Division is essentially in business to develop technology for licensing, which is somewhat unusual. But as a rule, the decision to license or to go into joint venture normally depends upon the stage of the technology, and how it is going to fit into one's own operations. If it is a piece of technology that is essentially usable at that time, then licensing is probably an option. If it is going to require some development, a joint venture is better because one can guide it in the direction that one would like to see it go. We actually do some joint venturing even in the development of technology for licensing.

Question for Dr. Good: If we were all more aware about the presumed virtues of licensing, how could that be used to boost general growth in R&D?

DR. GOOD: Some companies use the licensing of employee inventions to boost employee morale. If an idea is really good and it looks as if it has licensing potential, arrangements will be made for the employee to either share in the licensing profit or to continue to develop it in contemplation of a bonus.

By the way, a lot of off-line technology is developed in our laboratories. Nobody ever hears about it because we don't license it and we don't talk about it. And the reason that people do not license it is that they don't put enough time and effort in it to get it to the point where it has a demonstrable value to a licensee. To show that money can be made from a license, one must be able to show that the technology has some value to potential licensees.

There are lots of opportunities, I think, if people just look at them.

Another opportunity is to license some borderline technology through the vehicle of a joint venture.

Recently I had a conversation with people at a utility company in the Chicago area. They figured that their researchers were coming up with a lot of good ideas, but the company did not use them. So a little organization within the company has been set up to handle those ideas. If an idea appears to have some potential value, they make a decision whether to license it right off the patent. This is relatively inexpensive for the licensee, because a lot of work still has to be done to use it. If it is something that looks really promising, the organization puts a little more effort into it and gets it up to the point where it can provide a service to go with it and license an almost-ready-to-go package. The utility has been able to earn a fair amount of income just by reviewing what it already owns.

Question for Dr. Good: How do you arrive at an estimate for how much R&D a licensee should do? Is it some fraction of the income from the license? Is there a formula?

DR. GOOD: The R&D costs, as a percentage of sales, is very high for a company that licenses because it is an R&D-intensive activity. If one is really going to sell licenses, first, one has to be at the forefront of technology, or they are not very valuable. Second, they have to be very research intensive; otherwise people would do it themselves, with their own in-house technology. I would say many such firms spend 30, 40, even 50, percent of sales for R&D.

Question for Dr. Good: As a member of the National Science Board, the governing body of the National Science Foundation, you have recently endorsed university-industry cooperative research centers. Do you find this position inconsistent with the fact that university ownership of patents is only 2 percent of the total?

DR. GOOD: The National Science Foundation is supporting several technology centers today, and we hope there will be a few more. They are set up essentially to exploit more vigorously the kinds of things that were discussed earlier with respect to university-industry relationships. Until two years ago, all patents that were issued from government-funded work all belonged to the government. This meant that they were valueless for the most part, since, unable to get an exclusive license, companies did not put development costs into exploiting the technology. Then a law was passed (University and Small Business Patent Procedure Act—Patent Rights, 1981, P.L. 96-517) providing that patents emanating from federally funded projects can be owned by universities. With this change, I think university ownership of patents is likely to grow.

Question for Dr. Greene: Would you please elaborate on what is meant by a worldwide project team and how it functions?

DR. GREENE: Conceptually, a worldwide project team is a multidisciplinary team that includes professionals in medicine, pharmacology, organic chemistry, and so on. If we have under license an asset from a foreign company, and we are planning to develop this asset for the U.S. or other major markets, we insist upon being the leaders of the project team. But the company whose asset we license has representation on the project team.

Question for Dr. Greene: In the long-term, what are the expectations of SKF labs for the licensing group? That is, what fraction of new pharmaceutical products are expected to be produced by licensing?

DR. GREENE: At the present time, the opportunities coming from abroad have increased considerably. What has changed is getting access to particular compounds. It is not just money alone. From time to time we enter into a joint research program. Our objective is to have at least one compound a year of some other company under license development.

Question for Dr. Greene: Would you comment on how you locate items available from foreign sources?

DR. GREENE: There are several ways. First of all, the patent literature. Second, the scientific literature. Third, and what I consider to be the most important, is travel contacts. I have a group of ten people; six researchers, five of whom are Ph.D's, and four licensing people. We travel continuously all over the world. That, basically, is the best source of information, because everybody else knows what is in the patents and what is in the scientific journals. I'm after those things that have not appeared in public.

Question for Mr. McCloskey: Can you speak about limited partnerships in R&D?

MR. McCLOSKEY: Bruce Merrifield, the Assistant Secretary of Commerce for Productivity, Technology and Innovation, has proposed a model for limited-partnership joint ventures. He feels these afford an excellent opportunity. They are consonant with the antitrust laws and permit a company to do some off-balance-sheet financing of R&D. The idea is to get limited partners who would share with the company in the success of an R&D venture and who also have take-or-pay contracts with interested people.[1]

He says about 10,000 such limited-partnership joint ventures have been constituted. But they are not really for joint research in the classical sense. They are normally

---

[1] In take-or-pay contracts, the partners contract "in advance with companies or other organizations to buy or use [take] the results of the technology" on the condition that "the technology meets predefined specifications for cost and performance." (Source: U.S. Department of Commerce.)

designed to accommodate a company that wants to find an off-balance-sheet financing vehicle for specific research. I think he would say that it is not necessary to have a take-or-pay with that company. One organization might act as a general contractor for several limited partners, companies agreeing to pursue a definable goal—the development of million-bit memory, for instance—and divide the ensuing product among themselves.

Question for Mr. McCloskey: Do cooperative R&D ventures put together by an independent company like Merrill Lynch pose an antitrust problem?

MR. McCLOSKEY: I think most of the arrangements have one take-or-pay client, as opposed to competitors getting together.

Question for Mr. McCloskey: How do participants in joint-research ventures "share the spoils"?

MR. McCLOSKEY: That, I suppose, is up to the ingenuity of people and their lawyers. But to survive the antitrust guidelines, there has to be a defined and reasonable period in which the participants have exclusive use—it may be two or three years. An agreement to license to others may follow. It can be on a royalty-bearing basis.

The issues are: the combined market share of the participants; how many other competitor joint-research ventures exist; and how viable they really are. If somebody is excluded from a joint-research venture involving firms with a collective 25 percent market share, there is danger. The excluded company has been harmed because it has lost some opportunity. It is this situation for which clarification of the law is needed.

Question for the Panel: Take a small new company, with a strong R&D leaning, such as Cetus or Genentech. Would you be better off buying an equity position in that company or giving it contract research to do?

DR. GREENE: First of all, anyone faced with this decision has to understand what one's company's ultimate objectives are. Is the company going to enter into an arrangement with the small firm to develop a line of products, or does it want to use the technology as an entree to some other area?

DR. GOOD: We actually have been looking at some issues just exactly like that. The question centers on how big one's own R&D potential is. An equity position in a small company is a long-term proposition in terms of significant returns from the investment. It can be profitable, depending upon how those things turn. But if the large company has a sizable R&D effort of its own, it has to ask whether $5 million spent at the rate of $1 million a year in its own laboratory would not do it more good.

DR. TOLBERT: We have followed both paths. If one is looking to buy time, an early window onto something, then an equity position probably provides more leverage.

But if the aim is to get a particular job done, then a contract is appropriate.

Question for Dr. Good: Do you have any techniques for estimating how much a licensee would have to invest in R&D after purchasing a license, even assuming fully developed technology?

DR. GOOD: Of course, that is one reason why the whole business of licensing is so difficult. For instance, the licensor may very well have developed that technology for one purpose, and the licensee may really want to use that technology in a different way. In that event, a bit of in-house work will have to be done. On the other hand, some of the technology that we license is deliberately developed for specific customers in specific applications. In this situation, very little in-house work has to be done. Obviously, we get much higher premiums for granting licenses that call for us to provide technology and attendant service and guarantees.

The secret from the licensee's viewpoint is to have enough technical expertise to make a sound decision about what to pay for a license because the price should reflect what it will have to do in-house. Some people get into difficulty because they license technology that they believe is essentially ready to go, but that still requires a lot of R&D for them to adapt it to their facilities or for their particular application. To protect both the licensor and the licensee, there should be first-class technical people on both sides of the discussion. If not, one side or the other will be very unhappy sooner or later.

Question for Dr. Good: What about protection for the licensor when the licensee significantly improves a technology by its own efforts?

DR. GOOD: The legal questions can get very tricky if the licensor holds seminal patent protection or a seminal patent position. What happens is that the amount of royalty decreases as the licensor's position in that technology becomes less important. There are a lot of suits on whose patent really is the controlling one in a particular technology that was improved by the licensee. I can't stress too much the importance of writing good agreements.

DR. GREENE: In the pharmaceutical business, it is now standard, for drugs studied on a worldwide basis, that the licensor is compensated not only for the primary indication for a license, but for anything else that develops from clinical studies. This usually is set by contract or licensing agreement.

Question for Dr. Greene: How do you set priorities for international development work?

DR. GREENE: When the decision is made that a compound is of sufficient interest from a development point of view, it is taken before the president of Worldwide Pharmaceuticals, who sets the priority in relationship to other outgoing development work. Keep in mind that once we take a product into development, we also commit resources for five or six years, or however long it takes to develop that product.

Question for Mr. McCloskey: There are many reasons for doing collective work, but in the electronic industry, particularly, one of the motivations obviously is the concern about competition from Japan. Can that be cranked into joint-research agreements within the confines of the antitrust law, which at the moment, as I understand it, requires open membership and licensing at reasonable rates for everybody? How can you use collective work in the electronic industries and yet somehow provide a stronger U.S. competitive position vis-a-vis Japan?

MR. McCLOSKEY: The two Japanese targeted areas in the electronics industry are microelectronics, primarily in the chip manufacture of the random-access memory and also in the microprocess area, and the fifth-generation computer. In the United States, the initial projects proposed by MCC were in computer-aided systems design and software productivity. So there are several inviting areas for joint research.

Under Assistant Attorney General Baxter's philosophy (which is not incorporated into law), if the participants in a joint-research enterprise together hold, say, 15 percent of worldwide market share, other competitors could be excluded. But the semiconductor industry cooperative is open to all the companies in that industry. And it is not intended to stimulate competitive joint-research ventures. I'd say Hitachi would have to be allowed in; I do not know if it would force its way in. I think the members of the cooperative would rather that Hitachi did not ask to be admitted.

Part VI
The Innovative Process: Management's Key Role

Chairman: Egils Milbergs
Director, Office of Productivity, Technology
  and Innovation
U.S. Department of Commerce

Chapter 18
Why America's Technology Leaders Tend to Lose

Richard N. Foster
Director
McKinsey & Company

Companies such as Du Pont, B.F. Goodrich, National Cash Register, and RCA, among many others, have all lost major markets and millions of dollars because of their failure to manage technology. That is surprising to many, because all four are well-managed companies and all were, before they lost leadership, at the forefront of current technology in their industries. They all were market-share leaders. They were also the low-cost producers and very close to their customers. In short, they were doing exactly what most business schools tell us we ought to be doing.

They also had one other common characteristic: They were clobbered over a period of five to ten years by new competitors with new technologies. For example, National Cash Register, the leading manufacturer of electromechanical cash registers, wrote off $140 million of inventory in the early 1970's because new electronics products shoved them into obsolescence.

B.F. Goodrich led the development of bias-ply tires in the United States. It drove its suppliers to come up with better raw materials, better tire cords, and better designs, and was clearly in the lead in 1976. Three years later, in 1979, there were almost no bias-ply tires supplied as original equipment on U.S. automobiles; they were all supplied with radial tires by the French company, Michelin.

If we go back to 1955, RCA Corporation was the leading manufacturer of vacuum tubes. It headed a list of the ten major manufacturers in the United States. When solid-state technology came along, RCA began an enterprise to get into it, but, for one reason or another, it did not take the effort seriously enough. By 1975, RCA was out of vacuum tubes and also out of the semiconductor business. So were the other nine producers of vacuum tubes. Thus in the 25 years between 1955 and 1980, all of the leading electronics manufacturers in the United States ceased to be significant competitors in solid-state electronics.

These are dramatic stories. But they are not uncommon. If we focus on a small slice of time, we mainly see gradual change. If we focus on a little larger slice of time, as we have just now, we find that revolutionary change is more the order of the day.

Characteristics of Technological Change

What happened? We believe there are several unshakable "facts" about technological change that explain why these companies went wrong.

The first is that technological change underpins the competitiveness of many industries and companies much more than we realize. It is certainly the route to greater value for the customer in many instances because it enhances products and product features. It is also the route to lower-cost production and improved margins. Finally, it can reduce required assets and improve return on investment.

Technological change has, of course, been critical to high-technology industries, such as computers and telecommunications, but it has also fueled change in so-called low-technology industries. The revolution in automobile tires that has been mentioned, mini-mills in the steel business, changes in the packaging industry (from the two-piece can to the three-piece can), and the whole revolution in plastic packaging of food—these are just a few examples of how technological changes have really fueled the competitiveness of individual companies, indeed entire industries.

The second fact is that technological change within a given area of technology cannot go on forever. All technologies have their limits. Some are set by the laws of nature, such as the yield of a chemical reaction, fiber strength, and computer speed. There are also limits set by current industrial capability. For example, the thermodynamic efficiency of automobile engines is set by the strength and melting point of the metals used; the Japanese are experimenting with ceramic liners that will allow higher combustion temperatures. So, whether for scientific reasons or for present-day technological reasons, technological change cannot go on endlessly.

The third point is that the closer one is to these limits the more expensive it becomes to improve the technology. In technological development, the economics clearly indicate diminishing returns. Our experience suggests that it is ten times more expensive to advance technology that is reasonably close to its limits than it is to advance one that is only half way there.

Tire cords are used to strengthen tires and give them stability. In the early 1960's the primary cord was nylon. We have calculated that just about the time Celanese came out with polyester tire cords, it cost Du Pont between five and ten times more to make an equivalent amount of technological progress with nylon. The smaller company, Celanese, could invest $1 million and still remain competitive with Du Pont, which might have been spending $7 million. The example is even more dramatic than that, because Celanese was working on a product that had inherently better qualities than the Du Pont product. Du Pont ultimately lost the battle to a smaller competitor.

This phenomenon stands in opposition to the learning curve, which postulates that the more one does, the better one gets at it. In technology, the more one does, the worse one gets at it, not because the efficiency of what is being done is not increasing (because it is), but just because it is harder to solve the very tough problems that emerge in approaching the end of the technology curve.

The fourth fact is that when these limits are approached, it not only becomes more expensive to carry out technology development, but frequently technological discontinuities occur. As it becomes more expensive for one manufacturer to advance a technology, another manufacturer sees a different route that is much more economical. Celanese saw polyester while Du Pont was fighting with incremental advances in nylon. That is an incentive for new entrants to come into the business, and often they do. When it was becoming very expensive to improve vacuum tubes, the solid-state revolution came along. When it was becoming expensive to develop bias-ply tires, radials came in. When it was expensive for Smith-Corona to develop a little hammer font on its electric typewriters, IBM came out with its golf balls, and subsequently daisy wheels replaced golf balls. Low-pressure chemical processes have begun to replace high-pressure processes. In all these areas we find that as the limit of one technology is approached, somebody someplace figures out another way and then moves ahead.

Why Leadership Changes Hands

When these technological discontinuities appear, strategic leadership changes hands. That is the key point.

There are a couple of reasons for this. Many companies do not make the strategic decision to adopt the new technology in the first place. Of the top ten manufacturers of electronics in 1955, about half decided not to get into solid-state devices. The other half, however, did decide to get in. But it is difficult for a company that has managed one technology to learn how to manage a second. Skills are different; the economics of the business is different; the power structures in the corporation are different. There are enough differences to make it very difficult even for well-motivated people to overcome these cultural problems. Indeed, it is the cultural problems that are the restricting factors in technological change in the long run, not the inability to make strategic decisions.

The next part of the argument is that if management waits for the economic indicators of progress in its business to reveal the real problem, it will probably have waited too long. Markets are still growing, and that growth covers up the deterioration of the company's technological competitiveness. So management does not see it in the conventional economic indicators. The situation is further disguised because competitors rarely attack one another in major market segments at first. They attack in adjacent markets. When Michelin came into the U.S. radial market, it first went into off-the-road vehicles, not passenger tires. Goodrich may have said: "Why worry about off-the-road vehicles? That's just a small niche." It was not until Michelin went into truck and then passenger tires that Goodrich took notice, and by then it was too late.

Further deterioration of the business, when it comes, occurs rapidly. This talk about gradual evolution taking place in business just does not hold water. In fact, the deterioration of competitive position usually occurs much too quickly to allow management to retrace its steps and fashion a defense. We have looked at industry after industry and have concluded that it takes between four and seven years for one competitor to drop from 80 percent market share to 20 percent market share because of technological discontinuities. This is just as true in commodity chemicals as it is in semiconductors. That is too short a time for a company to decide to get into a new product line, and develop the people, skills and market reputation to be competitive.

If sales are declining in six or seven years, profits are probably declining to a negative position in two to three years. That's why NCR lost $140 million, why DuPont ultimately dropped out of the tire cord business, and why RCA, GE, Sylvania and Westinghouse, all of them initial entrants in solid-state technology, dropped out. Another reason why economic indicators are inadequate is that attacks often come from apparently "weak" competitors. In 1958, when Boeing introduced the commercial jet, the company was almost bankrupt. Lockheed and McDonnell Douglas, aware of the English experience with the commercial trial of the Comets, were very skeptical of Boeing's chances. But Boeing had only one choice. The only way it could compete was by moving into commercial jets—and it did so successfully.

The last element of my argument about why leaders lose is that defensive strategy designed to protect comfortable positions is rarely effective in doing more than buying extra time. Not that buying extra time is not important or economic, but it does not avoid the ultimate demise of the business. This is a form of economic protectionism. It is impossible to stave off the inevitable improvement in economic value that can be brought from technological change.

One of the most interesting examples of this is found in the ocean-transport business of the 19th century. Sailing ships dominated the high seas in the 1850's. Around that time steamships were introduced, and sailing-ship manufacturers scoffed at the new technology. But while they did, they entered into a program of what we would now call research and development. The typical sailing ship of that time had three masts and maybe four sails. Within ten years, it had four masts and five sails; and in another ten years, it had six masts and five sails. By the 1890's, they were up to seven masts with as many as fifty-five sails. These sailing ships were really marvelous things to see. Unfortuntely, not much ocean transport is carried by sail these days. Technological discontinuity was postponed for awhile, but eventually sailing ships disappeared from the horizon.

We have a lot of "sailing ships" around today. Some are called vacuum tubes. In 1968, RCA was still coming out with new lines of vacuum tubes called "Nuvistors." They were advertised as combining new materials, processes and functions. That was three years after IBM introduced the 360 machine, which had medium-scale integration, and just a year or two before it introduced the 370, which was the first large-scale integrated machine. The electronics revolution was on, but more vacuum tubes were still coming out of the laboratory. But few people chose to use vacuum tubes. In one case, it was RCA's black-and-white television, which went out of business a year later. RCA then ended up going to Japan and licensing technology for both semiconductors and color television.

A typical defensive move that companies make is market segmentation. This is a terrific way to get more value out of your customer population and is good business for the short term. But market segmentation can be a sign of technological maturity, and a sign that the business may be ready for discontinuity. Extensive focus on process-cost reduction, another sensible thing to do, may also be a sign of oncoming maturity.

Defensive R&D is the top priority in many large corporations. It, too, is a wise thing to do, *unless* it replaces offensive R&D—and in many firms today it does. Getting close to the customer is terrific, but if somebody else has a better product that provides more value, they will get the business. Customers are not that loyal.

Then there is the old approach of developing the technology and killing it in the company's own labs. That is not done much anymore, but it was for a while, and was terribly inefficient because other people always found ways of getting around to those technologies.

These troubles have plagued management in the past and are certainly going to be present in the future. Computers, telecommunications, electronics, most manufacturing operations, chemicals, drugs, agricultural materials suppliers and service companies, banks and insurance companies, arbitrators, lawyers, consultants, even antiques dealers, are going to be vulnerable to technological change in the next 15 years. We are sitting on top of a cornucopia of technological output and the thing to do is to take advantage of it, not try to fight it.

The new ventures have already started, although—in typical fashion—fairly silently. How many people know Teknowledge, Cognative Systems, Robotic Vision Systems, Monoclonal Antibodies, Inc., Cytogen Corp., Intermagnetics General, Superocon? These are all companies that are operating in hot areas of technology in small market niches, just as Texas Instruments was operating in small market niches in 1955 when it took on, preposterously, the giant RCA. Everyone knows what happened. Of course, all technologies start in niches—and many stay there.

Why Some Companies Retain Leadership

It is not inevitable that leaders lose, however, and there are positive examples. Harris Intertype Corp., an old manufacturer of linotype equipment, became Harris Corporation, relocated from Cleveland to Florida, and is now an electronics manufacturer. IBM, AT&T, Dow Chemical, Texas Instruments, are all companies that have a good batting average in technology. Even these companies can improve because it is hard for a large corporation to be consistent across all divisions at all times. However, by and large, they have done well. What do they do differently? First and probably foremost, they recognize that the end game of the competitive battle is set by the limits of technology. Each technology has its own inherent limits, and if management knows what those are for its technologies and its competitors' technologies, it is in good shape.

Second, these companies have learned not to rely on economic indicators of progress for their ultimate decision making. They have developed other indicators, based more on the *progress* of the technology than on conventional economic indicators. They know when to begin the development of a new technology. They also know that this step usually comes early in the game, because they recognize that the real determinant of change is the ability to change their culture, not their decision to change technologies. Management can make the latter change almost any day if it is prepared, but it can't change the culture overnight. It needs to begin early.

These companies have learned to recognize the signs of decay: discomfort with R&D output, finer and finer market segmentation, new competitors entering, weak competitors doing "crazy" things. These companies take all competitors, no matter how small, very seriously. They try not to fall into the trap of analyzing why competitors cannot succeed, but instead figure out the consequences if they do succeed. After all, that is where the real risk lies.

These companies have the courage to hold off capital investments in old areas of technologies and have pumped money into new areas, either by themselves or in novel combinations with others. Pratt & Whitney is entering a five-company consortium of international companies to develop the next generation jet for 150-passenger commercial planes. IBM bought into Intel to get better access to semiconductor technologies.

Remember when IBM was making its big move from centralized to decentralized computers and Wall Street disapproved, punishing IBM's stock price; IBM said, in effect, that it did not care—and blasted ahead. Time has proven IBM right. One needs this kind of courage to move ahead.

These companies understand short-term risk, but they also understand that minimizing short-term risk may mean maximizing long-term risk. The ever-present tendency to optimize present operations just entraps them. A company has to be ready to step out and change its base skill.

The better companies recognize this and deal with it accordingly. They seek a very close tie between the chief executive officer and the chief technical officer. The Conference Board recently asked CEO's who are their most trusted advisors? In only one case out of four was the chief technical officer listed.[1] My colleague, Ken Ohmae, who manages McKinsey's operations in Japan, estimates it would be eight cases out of ten there. I think this is the fault of both the CEO and the chief technical officer. Unless that relationship is nurtured, technology is never really going to be an integral part of strategy—matrices and other linking devices notwithstanding.

Top management in companies that stay ahead technologically lead by leadership, not by administration. They recognize the importance of vision, and the CEO takes a personal stake in figuring out what new areas of technology are going to be important. Because of the uncertainties involved there are inherently judgmental decisions. Such companies have the will to change. When George Dively changed Harris Intertype into Harris Corporation, it was a 15-year struggle. He did it with unusual single-mindedness.

Finally, it is very important to stay humble in this business of managing technology. We're not trying to bat 1,000. We are just trying to move from, say, 200 to 300, because if we can bat 300 we will probably have a pretty good shot at the World Series. And that is a lot better than most of us have right now.

[1] Ruth Gilbert Shaeffer and Allen Janger, *Who Is Top Management?* The Conference Board, Report 821, 1982.

Chapter 19
An Innovator's Perspective

John A. Bridges
Vice President, Research and
  Development
Aladdin Industries, Inc.

A great deal has been said about how American technology has slipped in the last few years. The statistics have been well documented: low R&D expenditures as a percentage of GNP; fewer engineers and scientists in R&D, as compared with other fields; and fewer U.S. patents granted to U.S. inventors. Ten years ago, 80% of U.S. patents granted were granted to American inventors. Today, this has dropped to less than 60 percent. This is not just disappointing, it is devastating for the economy. A frightening number of major U.S. industries are behind in technology as compared to the Japanese. Even in the fields where we are still out front, our lead is shrinking. What is going wrong?

It may be fashionable to blame the Federal Government, high taxes, rigid antitrust laws, environmental and safety rules, or even the recession. But I believe the problem is a lot closer to home than that. I think we in corporate management must take much of the responsibility; fortunately, corporate management also has the power to turn the situation around. To do this, however, we must understand the creative process and what makes innovators "tick."

Not a single one of the 75 patents that have been granted to me came as a result of top management's direction. They all came, however, as a result of top management's patience and encouragement. But I am lucky to work for a company where innovation is sought and encouraged. I am afraid this is not the general situation in our country today. In fact, I believe most corporations actually discourage innovation.

How to Encourage Innovation

One of the most disheartening problems to innovators is the standard corporate approach to the budgeting process. I agree with Peter Drucker's approach in his discussion of "The Operational Budget and the Opportunities Budget," in which he said, "both should be given the same amount of top management time and attention." The questions management asks of these two budgets are quite different. For the operational budget, one asks: "Is this effort and expenditure truly necessary? If not, how do we get out of it?" But if the answer is "yes" one asks: "What is the *minimum* needed to prevent serious malfunction?" For the opportunities budget, the first question is: "Is this the right opportunity for us?" And if the answer is "yes," one asks: "What is the optimum of efforts and resources this opportunity can absorb and put to productive use?"[1] I don't think many companies in this country follow Drucker's advice; as a result, our position of world leadership is gradually eroding.

Even if a company is fortunate enough to have separate opportunities and operational budgets, simple organizational problems can be terribly discouraging to the innovator. In his article, "How To Create Effective Change," Edward Emanuel wrote: "Divorce the innovating unit from the ongoing organization. Rules and procedures may be applicable and appropriate for what already exists, but they are meaningless in the creation of a new business, where false starts and setbacks are found to occur. In most cases, physical separation of the innovating unit from the ongoing organization is required."[2] He is suggesting that applied research be the group to improve existing products, correct mistakes, and expand the existing line. These projects can be

[1]Peter F. Drucker, *Managing in Turbulent Times.* New York: Harper & Row, 1980, p. 42.

[2]Edward E. Emanuel, "How To Create Effective Change." *Today's Manager,* November-December, 1976, p. 19.

planned to a large degree from the beginning of a year and can be measured by fairly objective techniques. Thus, applied research efforts should support the business unit strategies. There should be no pretense by the applied group that it is responsible for, or expected to do, long-range research. Individuals, however, should be given the freedom to "bootleg" without serious repercussions.

The other group to organize is the long-range or basic research group—or "opportunities" group, as Drucker called it. The people in this group should have *only* long-range projects in mind. No styling or simple line extensions should be accepted or tolerated. The main thing to consider here is people, rather than projects; that way offers the best chance for success. Unfortuntely, most companies spend their time, money and energy not on building new markets and generating wealth, but on what might be called share-of-market gadgeteering. What they try is to do the same thing—only a little bit better.

The long-range group can be organized in a variety of ways. One is the classic "think tank" operation. This has many advantages, but one disadvantage is lack of contact with the rest of the organization. "Think tank" people tend to take on an "ivory tower" or "egghead" image, and no matter how good their output, it is difficult to transfer their new ideas into the operational groups. One way around this is to use the venture-team approach. This was very popular with the matrix organizations of a few years back, and had the advantage of cutting across corporate organizational lines. One key point in making the venture-team approach successful is to pick a champion who is truly committed to the project, not just to keeping his job. Also, always get the best people available, not those who seem to be misfits with no other place to go.

Probably more important than any specific organizational approach, however, is establishing the best environment or climate for innovation.

- First and foremost is an attitude of optimism. The old "think positive" approach is an absolute necessity.
- Second, withhold early judgment. Don't worry about mistakes until they are about to cost a lot of money.
- Third, recognize the importance of the long-range effort, even though it is hard to measure. Give those people the prestige and support they need. Rotate the people as justified, making sure that the top creative people in the company are in these groups.
- Fourth, reward innovation well. Don't wait for absolute proof. Use judgment, and avoid tying bonuses to short-term financial results. Remember, a good idea can be identified only after the fact. A skilled innovator can make a lot of money for the company. Pay such a person accordingly and maybe he or she will do it for this company, rather than for another.

- Fifth, give ample freedom. Don't walk off and leave research people to do whatever they would like, but do give interest and encouragement. Do not rule with an iron hand.
- Finally, give the long-range group an adequate budget. We are talking about the future of a company: Today's good ideas are tomorrow's profits.

Project Selection

Once the long-range development group is organized with the best people and atmosphere, what should these people be working on? The biggest mistake could be simple jumping into "pet projects" on an ad hoc or random basis. I suggest that a fairly structured approach be used in preparing the innovative group for its task. This is not to say that the projects that they work on should be dictated, but, rather, that their education and indoctrination should be fairly well structured. Here are the steps I suggest to prepare the group for project selection: Have them conduct a survey of *company strengths*. Every member of the innovation team should completely understand the corporation's basic competencies. Look at the technology, the manufacturing, the distribution, the company image. By talking to the business-unit managers and the top executives in the company, see what they perceive as being the company's strong points. List them and make sure that everybody understands.

Taking this internal perspective may seem counter to the marketing philosophy. The marketing philosophy can imply that the market is everything, and that the manager must rigidly adapt internal resources to the outside world. Such rigidity is unnecessarily limiting. Instead, I suggest there should be a marriage between the firm's basic competencies and the markets.

After the group understands the company's strengths, be sure it *understands the company's strategies*. First understand the *divisions' strategies*. Some divisions or business units may not know what their strategy is. If so, propose one to them and see what kinds of arguments you get. A dialogue will eventually lead to a strategy statement. Even then, the division or business-unit managers may not agree with what they have paid to find out.

Turning to the *corporate strategy:* U.S. corporations have a curious addiction to corporate grand strategies. The Japanese approach could be called "strategy by hindsight." The bottom-to-top approach has often served them well, as opposed to the "grand vision" of the CEO, which guides many U.S. companies.

It is also important that the long-range group understands the special needs of the business. In deciding what to work on, it may be necessary to move toward a more balanced portfolio. Or the generation of cash and other such overriding considerations may need to be considered by the long-range group. As an example, if the company is blessed with a large herd of "cash cows," business opportunities should be developed to replace those "cash cows" as they age. Not to be ignored in the selection of projects and areas of interest are the heritage of the company and the opinions of the current top management. If the corporate culture is one of long risk and slow feedback, it would make little sense to consider risky research projects that would run counter to that culture.

Another prerequisite to consider before the long-range group actually engages in research projects is a study of trends, demographics and life-styles. This background gives the innovator perspective and improves the quality of the projects that are selected. Once this preparatory work has been done, the group can get to the real work of generating new product concepts.

A number of techniques can be used to generate ideas. But if the long-range group is not thoroughly prepared, its members are unlikely to come up with any "Eurekas" or flashes of genius. The skills of brainstorming, matrix analysis, context comparison, future wheels, and the like, should be mastered and understood as well as the normal skills that scientists and engineers are expected to possess. Creativity favors the prepared mind. Of course, all this is of no value unless there is a procedure in place to take good ideas and make a new business out of them.

Other Barriers to Innovation

No matter how well the long-range research group is funded, organized or prepared for its very important tasks, there will still be barriers to innovation. Probably the most difficult to overcome is *personality conflict*. The "not invented here" attitude of some managers and the lack of openness to new ideas can be truly difficult to deal with. Many times the innovator presents a personal image that is distasteful to top management and, rather than judging the quality of the idea, top management tends to judge the appearance or personality of the innovator—both of which are, of course, irrelevant.

There is another barrier when innovation is considered *too risky* compared with existing businesses. Research is often unpredictable. Most dramatic advances have not been the result of specific requests, but have been the result of imaginative exploration of new concepts. Some managers spend more time trying to avoid a mistake than simply trying something new. When compared with an existing business, most new ideas look rather anemic. If a company has 90 percent of the market and has the high profitability that such a dominant position implies, any candidate for a new product would be judged inferior. But as many major U.S. corporations have discovered in the last couple of years, this position can change rapidly. For many reasons, therefore, a balanced portfolio is extremely important to any corporation.

A third barrier to innovation is *executive compensation measured by annual financial performance*. This is too short term. The profit center mentality must be avoided at all costs in long-range development work. The riskier projects should not be killed by zealous operating managers with an eye on the next quarter's bottom line.

Another roadblock is new product *evaluation screening*. I am against any screening ratings, scores, financial return analysis, new-product evaluation teams, or any form of bureaucracy in the initial stages. The most successful new products will very often fall short in justifying investment in the early stages. Lack of patience with embryonic businesses will assure the demise of those businesses, since they are extremely fragile at that point. Good solid judgment by the CEO or the divisional managers is really all that is required.

Rigid control is yet another barrier. Most truly major developments defy the "planned approach." Most top managers, however, love control; that is how they got where they are. But this is not the way to foster new ideas. Corporate budget watchers usually insist on systematic progress toward some future completion date. Be careful lest some good opportunities be missed and some creative people be lost. Management by objectives works fine in many situations, but not in this one.

Another barrier is *lack of personal credit*. Giant corporations seem to take pride in keeping their creative people anonymous, giving most of the credit for the inventive genius to what they call "our research staff." My point here is that freedom of actions and credit for accomplishment are extremely important to creative people. If an inventor is making lots of money for the company, make that person the hero that he (or she) is.

Points to Remember

If you only remember a couple of things about innovation, I hope you'll remember these two:

First, divide your research activities into applied and long range. For the applied research people, ask for justification in detail, project by project. For the long-range staff, on the other hand, do just the opposite. Consider the people; get the best ones; and if they are productive, give them as much support as they will effectively absorb. These expenditures are generally "peanuts" in comparison to the rewards.

Second, budget adequately for innovation. There is no question that the ups and downs of business necessitate periodic adjustments of R&D budgets. But those adjustments should be made primarily in the applied-research area.

Our country is in trouble from a technological standpoint. We have no choice. We can't go on with the same old products; they will become obsolete and foreign competition will take away those that we still have. We *must* think long range.

Chapter 20
Questions and Answers

Question for Dr. Foster: You cited a number of examples of companies that lost their lead because of technological discontinuities. Are there examples of leaders who had been successful in navigating these discontinuities. If so, what characteristics were responsible for their performance?

DR. FOSTER: Let me mention again Harris Corporation, the former Harris Intertype Corp. of Cleveland. Harris Intertype was in the linotype business. Harris Corporation is a major electronics company. This profound change came about largely through strong leadership by the chairman, George Dively, who, around 1965, saw that the mechanical approach to typesetting could just not be significantly improved, but that the application of electronics might be promising. He had no specific design in mind for using such an application. He just had the faith, the vision I talked about, to back electronics as opposed to the conventional approaches.

What he did, then, was to stop investing capital in improvements of plant and equipment for the old technology. Instead, he bought a Melbourne, Florida, company called Radiation Inc., and made that the nucleus of his new activities. Today, Harris Corporation is headquartered in Melbourne, and 18 out of 20 SBU managers run businesses Harris Intertype did not have in 1965. It is that kind of vision, anticipation, leadership and will to change which is characteristic of companies that have dealt successfully with technological discontinuities.

I think IBM has had a very good record in going from centralized machines to decentralized machines, moving into personal computers. I think AT&T also has a very good record. With one million employees, the difficulty for AT&T to move into a new area is absolutely staggering. Yet it has done so, to its great credit. I think Corning has been successful in this regard with its various joint ventures—Owens-Corning Fiberglas Corp. for example. If these ventures had been kept internally, I doubt whether they would be nearly as successful as they are today.

Incidentally I very much support what John Bridges said about keeping the innovating organization separate. The companies I have mentioned have found ways to do that. This is another characteristic they share.

Question for Mr. Bridges: Would you say that your company has lost a good innovator in promoting you?

MR. BRIDGES: That is a dilemma. On the one hand, no matter how much one talks about the dual ladder, it is not quite the same as being right in the control tower. I've worked hard at trying to do more things than I would if I were back in the lab. But everybody has just 24 hours a day, and naturally I don't have as much time to spend on creative thought as on administration.

Question for Dr. Foster: How do you quantify the position of technology on the S-curve? And would you please comment on when and how the R&D organization should establish limits on the performance of current and developing technologies in order to stimulate the search for technological discontinuity?

DR. FOSTER: As to the position on the S-curve, three things have to be done. The first is to understand the appropriate measure of performance. It is not numbers of patents, numbers of new products, or anything like that. The measure of performance has to meet two conditions. First, it is relevant to the interests of customers and, to the extent that these are industrial customers, that means relevant to their economic interests. Sometimes that means capital-saving innovations; sometimes it means cash-saving innovations. Second, the measure of performance has to be one that can be influenced by technical means; if not, why worry about it?

The second thing to do is to determine the technology limit, or at least have a perspective on what that limit is. To do this one must first identify the limiting mechanism. Is it thermodynamics? It is kinetics? Whatever it is, its quantitative implications can then be determined. By the way, that turns out to be a fairly creative process. Different people will have defensible points of view on limiting mechanisms. Such a debate often will reveal that one is much farther from the limits than had been thought. The way to find that out is by addressing the limiting-mechanism question.

Once it has been established what we are measuring, and where the top of the curve is, presumably one knows today's position on the S-curve. The remaining question is to determine the slope of the S-curve. That is largely determined by the economics of development; these are affected by the adequacy of the knowledge base, the timing of the company's technological effort, the innovation, the aggressiveness of company objectives, its basic design capability, and so forth. These are company-specific. Through understanding historically what they have been, one can get some sort of projection for what they might be in the future. And now the S-curve is reasonably well-defined.

If the company is near the top, then the answer to the second question, when to start looking for the new S-curve, is "right away." The closer one is to the top, to the limits of present technology, the more urgent is the need to look for the new one. What does "look" mean? One way of looking is reading the magazines, keeping up with the technical literature. Another is having an exploratory research program. The right way to look is very dependent on the company's skills and the urgency of the need to look.

The difficulty of looking is that it will often take the searcher outside the conventional range of his or her technical skills. How does the polymer chemist look for advances in ceramics? How does a mechanical engineer look for advances in electronics? How does the solid-state digital engineer look for advances in software? How does a banker look for advances in electronics? These are very tough questions; the answer, I guess, is with diligence. Keep at it and develop some of these capabilities. And if the company is blind-sided, it's probably because of the inability to figure out the solution to this particular problem.

Question for Dr. Foster: Since most top-management people have not been in R&D and don't understand these signs, how does one communicate them?

DR. FOSTER: The management of technology is different from doing technology. Managing technologies, making the investment decisions, thinking about the key questions, is something that could and should be part of general business education and familiarity. And the kinds of principles we are discussing are very understandable by top managers, even though they do not master the details of technology or the specialized vocabulary, which is often a huge stumbling block. Banging away at those principles is probably more productive than banging away than at the ever-changing technology.

Question for Mr. Bridges: You mentioned that personality conflict is one of the barriers to creating an innovative culture. Suppose a personality problem is severe? Whose responsibility is it to deal with it?

MR. BRIDGES: It must be both parties' responsibility. The innovator certainly has to play the game. But top management has to be ready to compromise as well. With luck they meet somewhere in the middle.

Question for Chairman Milbergs: How can we maintain a continuous stream of scientists and engineers when the spigot is controlled by short-run economic conditions?

MR. MILBERGS: The federal role in supporting our scientists and engineers should be a long-term commitment. Right now, federal funds for R&D and the support of scientists and engineers are increasing while many other budgets are being reduced. And our programs are planned to have some duration. The 200 Presidential awards for young investigators will be a five-year program.

Industry has a big responsibility here. Training cannot give a person a lifetime skill. I recently visited General Dynamics' F-16 plant. The engineers and technical people there maintain that when someone has been out of school for four or five years, the basic skills learned there are obsolete. So they want to hire people with the attitude, character and the capacity to learn. The capacity to learn must be emphasized in our engineering schools, both undergraduate and graduate, since students will have to renew their skills continuously through their working lives. The government should play a role in this, but I hope the private sector also begins to exercise its influence on the educational establishment because, in the end, the private sector uses the product of that establishment. And if that product is not adequate, industry has to spend millions of dollars making it adequate—a tremendous waste of resources. If there is any area of productivity lag in this country, it is in our educational system.

MR. BRIDGES: Could I add a comment? Part of the educational problem that needs correcting is the curriculum of business schools. They are graduating many people who really have a big gap in their education. We can put out all the scientists and engineers we want, but if we still have businesspeople who think about business in administrative terms and don't understand the power of technology and some of the competitive implications, I think we are still going to be in trouble. I would like to see the business schools adjust their curricula to include the issues raised in this conference.

Question for Dr. Foster: Your comments seem to indicate that many U.S. industries are destined to be defenders while many foreign industries are natural attackers. Is this true? A related question: How do you maintain the advantages you have even though you are the defender?

DR. FOSTER: I don't think we are inherently on the defensive. I think we have the potential to be on the attack. The areas of science that are developing most rapidly in the world are moving fastest in this country—

software technology and biotechnology, to name two. We have a base here which is, I believe, second to none. By the way, "Japan, Inc." is not a single monolith attacking us. It is only 20 individual companies. There are a lot of companies in Japan that lose money, even though their employees also sing the company song every morning.

Our risk is that we spend too much time and energy trying to defend the old structure. And the economics of defense are terrible, as I pointed out earlier. It will cost us much more to defend than it will to attack. So let us put our resources into these new areas of technology. It is, in a sense, the 20th century equivalent of Adam Smith and free trade. Just as he was suggesting that we not put up barriers against countries that are the lowest-cost producers, so we also must not put up barriers to protect those industries that, because of the technology, are now inherently high-cost producers. We have substitutes for almost every product available in the United States. I can't think of a major market that will not be affected by one of the new areas of science and technology in place today. And if we can use that insight to foster the kind of discontinuities that we have been talking about, we will, in a sense, be attacking ourselves and, therefore, assuring our own survival.

MR. BRIDGES: I certainly agree with that. The attitude of optimism, as I said, is absolutely essential—although we have to be realistic, we can't sit back and talk about how bad things are and how much the Japanese have done. We are still the greatest nation and have the greatest technologies. If we keep fostering the new ideas, keeping the entrepreneurial spirit alive, we'll get there.

Part VII

R&D and Corporate Strategy
Chairman: Joseph G. Gavin, Jr.
President and Chief Operating Officer
Grumman Corporation

Introductory Remarks by Session Chairman Joseph G. Gavin, Jr.

I can't resist the opportunity to highlight some things mentioned earlier. One is leadership by top management. Top management must have the conviction that innovation is important. If it does not, everybody is in trouble, and the company will have less success than it should.

There are two other factors I would mention. One is desperation. In my experience, sheer desperation has produced the best innovative thinking. I'm not sure whether it is the pinch-hitter syndrome, or what it is, but it is amazing what people will do when something has to be accomplished, and rapidly. The second factor is luck. Sometimes things happen right. For example, in the 1950's we devoted a lot of time to working out a rather complex mathematical treatment for devising the optimum path for a high-performance airplane to climb from sea level to high altitude. At the time we devised these mathematical techniques, we had no idea that, with slight modification, they would come in handy two years later to give us the ability to compute optimum orbital transfers.

Chapter 21
Institutionalizing the Management of Technology

Martin Cooper
Vice President & Director of
   Research & Development
Motorola Inc.

First, some brief definitions:

Strategy consists of those boundaries and directions that are intended to distinguish a company from its competitors in order to foster successful prosecution of its businesses: the key issues that distinguish the company from its competitors.

Development is the application of scientific principles and knowledge to solve the problems of customers, to help them improve their productivity, to help them do things they could not do otherwise.

Research is the creation of these scientific principles and knowledge that are used by the developers.

Technology is what the developers develop. It is the application of scientific principles and knowledge to create products that benefit society. And in our organization we tend to equate the benefit to society by the profitability of those products to our company. We do not consider that products do much for society if they are not profitable.

About Motorola

Motorola is a technology-based company. Our products, whether they are hardware or services, involve the application of scientific principles, directed by our people, to solve the problems of our customers, to improve their productivity, or to let them do things they could not do otherwise. As a result, we have built a considerable skill in developing these products and in creating the processes that permit us to bring products to market. Our technological decision makers have been required to forecast changes in technology, to anticipate new ways of doing things, and aggressively to search for the means to render their existing products obsolete.

We have been pretty good at doing those things: Our success in the marketplace demonstrates that. But we observed over the years that our products and processes were becoming much more complex than before. It had become difficult, perhaps impossible, for a product manager, no matter how clever, to anticipate all of the technologies which could possibly affect the product. More important, we discovered that we were encountering similar problems in different parts of our company, but that we had become so large that the solutions were not being carried across divisional and geographic boundaries. Despite diligent monitoring by management, we knew that, on occasion, we were spending resources—people and money—to solve the same problem in two independent and noncommunicating laboratories. We discovered cases where solutions created within a specific laboratory would not necessarily find their way into a product line for no other reason than a lack of advocacy. Worst of all, there was the danger that, because we weren't disciplining ourselves to think far enough ahead in an organized way, we would neglect some important element of technology, some new technique, a process, a machine,—we would let our competitive advantage lapse as a result.

Making People Pay Attention

I would like to describe three tools that have helped us institutionalize the management of technology at Motorola. The intent of these tools is very simple: to make people pay attention. I would like to take issue with the thesis that the role of top management is to have vision. I don't think that is true any longer in most companies. There is nothing that legislates against the management having vision, but its real role is to get people to pay attention, to convince them, to encourage them, to pay attention to their technologies, both long range and short range.

Paying attention is harder than it sounds. We all know how vital it is to establish a balance between the efforts that our managers exert on their immediate problems—the achievement of their profit and loss goals and their reaction to current events in the marketplace—and their achievement of goals five years or more into the future.

There is great temptation for a manager of technology, or a business manager, to sacrifice some of the future on the altar of immediate performance. The tragedy of such sacrifices lies in the agony of recovery. When a new technology is neglected for a year or two, it is sometimes possible to catch up but then only at great cost, inefficiency and an uphill morale struggle. Wouldn't it be much better, we thought, if we could create a mechanism whereby the responsibility for maintaining the proper balance between today and the future could be spread among more of the experts in a business, not only the direct manager? Wouldn't it be exciting to establish a medium for exchange of solutions within the corporation? Wouldn't our lives be easier if we could have a glimpse of the future; a vision of our directions and alternative directions for the next five to ten years and longer? Wouldn't it be nice to anticipate the need for specific elements of technology so that our people could create them, so they could be ready when our product designers needed them?

The Technology Roadmap

Out of questions such as these arose the concept of the Technology Roadmap, which encourages managers to pay attention to their technological future and gives them a vehicle to organize their forecasting.

The specific format of the roadmap varies among our different businesses, partly because there are differences among the businesses but mostly because of the differences among the people who manage these businesses. That is not really important. The tool is theirs and they have a hand in creating it, in making it comfortable and useful, and in continuing to use it in their businesses. Furthermore, the tool should be accessible to all of the manager's people, so that an engineer or a marketer working in a very narrow area of the technology of a product can get the big picture, and can quickly grasp the whole product line.

There are some common elements and uniform techniques in the roadmaps, which are really a series of documents. They generally look backward to see where we've been, and ahead to predict where we're going.

When we look back, we are looking for a trend, a pattern, an historical context for our future prediction. Depending upon what we are examining, five years of history may be adequate, or a twenty-year look may be necessary.

As an example, we examine the life cycles of earlier products. Some of these product life cycles vary from six years or less to over twelve years. To get a picture of a repeating pattern, at least two full cycles should be examined—12 to 20 years of history. Yet most of our products exhibit the classical repeating pattern of slow growth at introduction, a fast growth as the marketplace recognizes the value of the product, a maturing as a market is saturated or competition catches up, and a phaseout as new products, we hope our own, render the old obsolete. From this life cycle we determine when development of the next generation of a specific product should start. Incidentally, it is generally true that the time to start working on the next generation is when the peak has been reached, before a specific product has saturated the marketplace. This is not, however, the characteristic perception of people in a product line. The tendency is, as has been mentioned, to wait until saturation has been achieved, or the curve starts declining.

Another essential part of the roadmap is the well-known experience curve. We have demonstrated repeatedly that our costs and prices follow a regular price reduction, proportional to cumulative experience. So we plot the history of our costs as a function of our cumulative unit shipments and the price as a fraction of industry shipments, determine the slope, the trend, and predict our future costs and prices.

When or if those two curves converge, of course, the product will not be making money. But if this prediction is made soon enough, it will be apparent that cost-experience efforts are not adequate, that the cost curve will have to be tilted downward. This enables management to set believable cost-reduction goals. The value of the experience curve and product life cycles in the management of technology cannot be overemphasized—although people generally do not at first believe them. The usual response for a product manager is that the experience curve is a wonderful thing; the product life cycles are great; but they really do not apply to this product, because this product is different. He or she can cite chapter and verse in support of this view. But we have not found any situation where the product life cycles and the experience curve are not applicable, interesting and revealing.[1]

Predicting technology trends—another element of the roadmap—can be equally organized and scientific, but

[1]Roadmaps also commonly include S-curves. For a description of S-curves, see pages 79-80. While life cycles and experience curves relate to specific products, S-curves usually relate to broad technologies or purposes.

varies more from business to business. Our integrated-circuit people can project trends of the number of devices on a chip of silicon and the speed and power of their circuits. Our mobile-communications people may examine the number of people they can serve in a given width of frequency spectrum and the ability of their receivers to reject interference—once again extrapolating history.

As we produce each of these projections, it is important to be reminded that our competitors can profoundly affect our plans. To learn everything we can from their actions, we will duplicate many of the historic analyses for our competition and will, in effect, create a technology roadmap to anticipate their actions. In actuality, the competitive roadmap may consist only of our own entries, but it is as important to analyze competitive price-experience curves and product cycles as it is our own, and to use these and other tools to predict their future movements.

These are logical, organized tools. The next step requires a bit more creativity and more expertise and judgment. It is necessary to predict the changes, the breakthroughs, the *new* devices or processes or tools which will become useful in our future. The expertise to make these predictions exists throughout our company: The challenge is to draw the predictions out of the engineers and scientists, marketing specialists, managers, manufacturing technologists—we even think we should be talking to psychologists and anthropologists. The challenge is also to extract the adversary positions and to be sure that they flavor our image of the future. One of the methods we use to encourage debate will be discussed below.

The next step in the process of creating and maintaining the roadmap involves bringing together the roadmaps of all of our relevant businesses to be sure that they mesh. Are the equipment designers projecting the right integrated-circuit cost and density? Are the integrated-circuit people projecting the advances in process equipment as aggressively as the unit of the company responsible for making and marketing that equipment?

As comprehensive as it is at this point, our technology roadmap is still not finished. We now have a plan for the future of our products. We have an educated judgment of what they will sell for, what they have to cost so we can maintain profitability in our business, what customer features and manufacturing technologies and device technologies will be needed. We know about when we will have to announce each generation to maintain the growth of our businesses and to stay ahead of our competitors. Thus, we know when we have to start the development programs that will result in these product announcements. We have established milestones of progress on each of the measures I have mentioned, and we can manage to these milestones; we can establish priorities for our programs; and we can intelligently decide where we can best invest our technological resources, our people, and facilities, to get the best impact on our businesses.

There is one more step, and that is to prepare the basic technologies, the ones that have to be ready before we can even start our development programs. We should be able to set priorities for our research programs and establish their goals and milestones. We now have the vision and confidence to fund these programs and to insure that this funding continues even as short-term fluctuations occur in our various businesses or in the whole economy. Corporate management can have intelligent visibility of the advanced, research-oriented technology as well as the immediate product technology and can insure that an overzealous product manager will not sacrifice 1989 product superiority to improve 1983 profits by delaying a vital research program.

The technology roadmaps at Motorola have become fundamental tools for most of the people upon whom we depend for our products and technology. While we corporate managers regularly review the roadmap and the product strategies, the roadmap is their tool to help them run their businesses, as we regularly remind them. They maintain and revise and expand it. The only corporate caveat is that they may not change the scope of a program without involvement of the corporate staff.

The Long-Range Technology Planning System

Yet the roadmap is not without flaws. One is bulk. Every business has a roadmap that is several inches thick. This makes us worry about having created a bureaucratic mechanism.

A second, more significant, flaw is that we still have not persuaded people to look beyond the generation of products following today's products. They do need a vision still further into the future. So we have overlaid a second system that we call the long-range technology planning system. We identified 115 specific technologies in which the Motorola Corporation is engaged (we are an electronics company; the number would be different for companies in other industries), and we picked out for study those technologies that were the fastest moving, that had the greatest uncertainties, that gave us concerns. For each technology that we wanted to study, we constituted a steering committee made up of experts from throughout the company. Each steering committee was given four charges: first, to understand what is being done in Motorola with the technology in question; second, what competitors are doing, what is happening in the rest of the world; third, to compare one and two and determine whether the company was achieving its objective (and the objective is always leadership); and, finally, to make recommendations to the corporation about what should be done to correct the problem, if there were one, or otherwise to change things. Corporate reactions include corporate funding of business programs, having the corporate R&D laboratories work on the technology, doing nothing (but this is rare), and other measures.

The Technology Review

But do the technological roadmap and the long-range technology planning system mean that people are going to do the things that we encourage them to do? The answer is no. One can ask people to do things, can explain why, but if one does not keep explaining, and does not bring the urgency of action to their attention in some forceful ways, they will not respond. Here is what we have done at Motorola. This may be the key point I make: Top management pays attention and everyone knows it.

The manifestation is that every business in the corporation is reviewed at least once a year by top management in a mechanism called the technology review. It is generally an all-day meeting, though for smaller businesses it may last only half a day. Both the president and the chairman of the board participate in almost every one of these technology reviews; one of them participates in *every* review; and some of the reviews involve the chairman, the vice chairman, and the president.[2]

During these reviews we quickly come to an overall understanding of the business, the marketing environment, sales growth, and profitability. We then go through the technology roadmap, get an update on anything new that is happening, give the adversaries an opportunity to present their positions, and, in general,

---

[2]Motorola's Chief Executive Office recently, after seven years, delegated management of the Technology Reviews to sector managers. The Chairman, Vice Chairman, and President continue to attend the reviews.

have an exchange of ideas on the status of the technology of that business. It is a participative meeting. The important thing is that product managers know that the chairman of the company and the president examine their technology roadmaps—which are now living documents—at least once a year, and often twice a year in businesses that are volatile. They know that top management is paying attention.

A Salubrious Environment

We think we are now building an environment where a proper balance is maintained in the amount of attention our people pay to short-range versus long-range issues, to operating versus strategic matters, and to technology versus the many other professional disciplines which must be managed in a successful company. The technology roadmap, the long-range technology planning system, and the technology reviews have turned out to be valuable and exciting tools in helping us create this balance.

Experience Curve for Quality

Mr. Cooper offered obiter dicta about quality in the manufacturing process:

"We discovered that trying to establish a fixed, single-value quality goal is not feasible, because the goal must be continued improvement. So we plotted experience curves for quality, a very valuable tool. The experience curve may be defects per million for a semiconductor; it may be percentage of failures for a piece of equipment. Whatever the measuring stick, we found that there is in fact a linear relationship between time and quality. We now have the ability to predict, and we ask people in the various product lines to predict, their quality achievements in the future, to state the steps they will have to take to maintain quality leadership in their markets."

Chapter 22
Corporate Direction and R&D

Lewis M. Branscomb
Vice President & Chief Scientist
International Business Machines Corporation

The Chief Scientist of IBM is the chairman of the Corporate Technical Committee, which has six members, four of whom are appointed on one-year, full-time assignment to our corporate headquarters. Our job is to influence the long-term scientific and technical direction of the enterprise for its overall well-being. We are part of the corporte office, or, as it is now called, the Corporate Management Board. We also have a Science Advisory Committee, a group of outside-the-company academic consultants on retainer who give us an external perspective.

The discussion in these papers comes down, I think, to the role of the CEO and the extent to which that individual can manage the technological future of the company based on his common sense, the extent to which he needs to have technical expertise or needs to develop special ways of managing those who do have the technical expertise.

Strategies for Research, Technology and the Business

The issue being discussed is technology strategy. It is important to distinguish that from research strategy, which is fairly simple. Research strategy guides the research labs' efforts to prepare for the future. The distinction between technology strategy and business strategy is sometimes lost. Business strategy, of course, is the means to achieve one's financial goals, expressed in product or service opportunities. Usually business strategy is developed in relation to an understanding of competitive products and services and prices. Technology strategy is a means to achieve business goals. It is much more difficult to define because it is much more heavily affected by external influences than is research strategy.

First of all, a competitor's technology strategies and capabilities are harder to predict than its product plans. The latter are usually implicit in the competitor's current activity and in its customer set. Indeed, the competitor's technology strategies and capabilities are subject to the same uncertainties that each of us faces in determining the future technical capabilities and directions of our own companies.

Second, one's technology strategy is clearly limited by the art of the possible, as Mr. Foster indicated. At IBM we have an explicit way to deal with this limit. Our corporate research organization identifies all the major technologies on which our business depends—electronic logic technology, for example—and always has two major projects in place for each technology. One is aimed at determining what limits nature sets to the improvement of current mainstream technology. For electronic logic, that would be silicon electronic-circuit technology of ever smaller dimensions. The second project is aimed at the single most promising radical alternative—the next S-curve or two, as Mr. Foster has described the process of innovation. For electronic logic, that would be superconducting Josephson technology or, perhaps, gallium arsenide technology. Thus we try to have knowledge of where technical limits are—knowledge that is quantitatively expressed and based on actual research—in order better to understand the limits of our business possibilities.

The time horizons for technology strategy and business strategy may not always be in synchrony. They may be the same, or it may not be clear which is the longer. One's business strategy may have a long time-horizon. As Jack Goldman of Xerox is fond of pointing out, the buggy-whip manufacturer of the early 1900's might not be out of business today had management realized that it was in the vehicle accelerator business. In this example, one sees a long-term business strategy; the technology and product strategies are the independent variables.

Other companies may in fact, have a technology-driven strategy, as most of the U.S. semiconductor industry has had, or perhaps even a manufacturing-driven strategy, to which that industry is being driven because of the enormous increase in costs and complexity of the manufacturing facilities for its products. For a manufacturing-driven strategy, product, pricing and marketing strategies have to be derived from the manufacturing plan in order to maintain full loading of the manufacturing facilities. As manufacturing gains a more technological cast, companies will find themselves more and more driven by manufacturing strategies, with the product technology being embedded in the manufacturing strategy. I think that is what the Japanese have often done, and done very well indeed.

But, of course, many businesses with well-defined visions of their long-range futures, are driven by product or business *case* strategy. Here we come to a dilemma for those firms confronting an environment where business conditions are changing very fast, where product technology and marketing conditions are changing rapidly. It is precisely in this environment that one wishes to have a business-case driven strategy to ensure that one is responsive to the marketplace. Yet a business-case driven strategy makes it hard to have a technology strategy with enough staying power to be successful, because, as Mr. Foster pointed out, continuity is an absolute requirement for an aggressive technology strategy. It takes time to develop the skills and the programs to bring about wholly new capabilities.

So in Dick Foster's metaphor of a war, in which he gives the edge to the attackers, it seems to me that metaphor makes the assumption that the defender cannot release itself from its past in order to be an attacker itself. What this means is that propensity to change is probably as important as having aggressive technological plans or aggressive business plans.

Of course, both are required. But from management's point of view it is often as hard to foster change as it is to foster committed effort to long-term innovative activities. And internal change may be essential to the ability to take advantage of such activities.

Seven Levels of Activity

I would like to take slight exception to the impression possibly left by others that a given business moves from S-curve to S-curve after examining the situation at some appropriate point on one curve and deciding that it is time to go to the next one. This examination, I believe, is inevitably a continuous process, at least in those industries where product lives are in the four-to-five year range or less, because the time required to carry through

a major innovation or a major cycle of the business is substantially longer than that.

I think of IBM as simultaneously engaged in seven levels of activity at all times. We are managing all seven simultaneously, and there is no discrete decision to jump from the first to the second. We are moving from one to seven and our whole product line is in a state of overlap.

To illustrate: We are *maintaining* in the field machines such as our 3033 (level 1); we are *selling and installing* (level 2) the newer 3081's and 3084's (installing those machines is a major technical effort); we are doing the *manufacturing, engineering, testing and the preparation for production* of the family of yet-to-be announced machines (level 3); we have development teams engaged in *design and technology* of the next (fourth) level of products and technology. We have *advanced technology projects* to size, conceptually, a fairly well-defined product line (level 5).

Our research division is primarily *committed to concepts* for use in the sixth level of technology. And, of course, the more basic-research people in this division are *working on the limits of the technology* that will determine the nature of the seventh level of machines, or the kinds of technology strategy that might produce it.

So the whole IBM community is involved, to some extent, in all seven levels of products. There are interactions among the levels because one gets to the future from the past. The way in which our customers are now using the 3033's in the field determines to a substantial degree the characteristics of the next family of machines. As has been pointed out, product architecture or computing-machine architecture is not like building architecture. When an architect designs a building, he starts out with the client's requirements; he prepares a plan, does the engineering, and then the contractor starts to build. But we always have to remember that our customers are already living in the building that we are trying to design.

With seven levels of technology, spaced about two years apart, we are dealing with fourteen or more years of technology history, going about six years into the past and eight or more into the future.

Development versus Research

Notwithstanding their interdependence, at IBM we see development and research as quite distinct activities. Our development planning derives from a business-case discipline for specific products. Each product plan has its own development plan and its own development resources are determined. Of course, that is done in the hindsight of the ratio sheet that shows what is typical, and it is done in the context of the strategic technology and production considerations covering our factory plans and coming technology. And of course it is done in the knowledge that there are staffing strategies and facilities limitations that must be faced if one contemplates major excursions from past experience. But it is a microeconomic process. Our operational planning system is really the mechanism for bringing internal consistency to all of the business decisions once or twice a year. It is not a corporate development plan that is dispensed to the divisions. I do not think we are different from most other companies in that respect.

We manage our research investment very differently. Research investment is based on a business judgment by top management, not on a computed economic return. We do not attempt to apply economic business-case tests to our research division. We do, of course, look at its track record; "What have you done for us lately?" is a perfectly reasonable question. It also puts on research the responsibility to try to make sure that its work is used by the business units. That technology transfer is very important.

The research strategy, then, is generated independent of the business operating plan and with some independence from the strategic technology direction. One of the principal responsibilities of the Corporate Technical Committee is, however, to review both our research strategy and our technology strategy to ensure that they are appropriately interrelated.

The Role of Planning

I've implied that the purpose of operational planning is not to make business decisions so much as it is to test the consistency of decisions. This is even true in strategic planning to a considerable extent. Of course, IBM, like every other company, makes business decisions whenever they are ready to be made. And having made a business decision in March, we know that it is likely to be incompatible with the corporate plan that was accepted in January. The "plan of record" is therefore an important base line. It quickly becomes incompatible with the actual decisions that have been approved, because business decisions are made whenever they need to be made. The process of resetting the corporate operating plan is, of course, a major activity that we carry out once a year.

The planning system, then, is expected to expose the dependencies of one unit of the company on another; to expose assumptions about the external environment; and to facilitate the resolution of debates between line and staff about the realism of those assumptions, or of debates between line and line about interdependencies.

We can also use planning as a challenge to conventional thinking and to subject visions of future opportunities to disciplined analysis. One component of our planning is management's semiannual review aimed at the business outlook ten years out. This is a most important exercise, because one needs to make a model for the business potential for the whole industry, worldwide, ten years hence, and then test the plausibility of one's own business objectives. Unless one tests the plausibility of corporate goals with some detail of analysis, then the assertion that we intend to grow as fast as the industry might lack the credibility it requires.

Managing Failure and Success

Managing both risk and opportunity is very important in strategic technology management. Many companies take risks; few manage failure very well. The management of failure consists of three significant elements. First is managing the careers of the people who are responsible at the time of a failure. It is necessary to understand the causes of the failure. One does not reward failure, but one must resurrect the careers of those who have been taken out of their previous jobs when a business disappointment requires restructuring of the organization. Many such people in IBM have, in fact, gone on to very successful careers. When that message is read throughout the company, it helps keep managers willing to set the goals high and commit themselves to rapid technical progress.

Second, one must learn and profit from mistakes to exploit what was positive in the failure. For some of our greatest successes, the key technology elements came from unsuccessful projects from which we extracted technology of great importance.

Third, management of failure requires that failure is made tolerable. It may be all right for a very large project to fail, although, as a member of our Corporate Technical Committee once remarked: "It is OK to have an Edsel division within a company, but it isn't OK to be the Edsel Company." The point is: Maintaining alternatives is important. If something radical and new is being attempted, entailing a major company commitment, put one person in charge of keeping its predecessor going. The old horse may have a lot more mileage left in it than one realizes. And even if failure threatens the radical approach, don't abandon it hastily, either. The project may simply be premature. Timing is everything.

As for managing success, I am impressed that relatively few companies prepare upside strategic alternatives. But what happens if a new product or endeavor goes much better than expected? One needs to have a plan to move rapidly. Of course, an upset investment plan is rarely a problem if the company has been successful. But what may not have been thought through is the set of human skills needed to exploit an unanticipated advantage that requires rapid expansion.

Take the example of the personal computer. We did not know how well we would do when we went into that business. We moved quickly, from decision to production in one year. Success required a major capability in personal computer software. We purchased our software from vendors that had already proven they were competent in producing software for other products of that character. But something more might be needed if the personal computer did well. So we provided a generous purchase discount for employees and told those who bought our machine and used it at home that we would buy software from them and pay them a royalty just as we would pay an outside software vendor. This put between 15,000 and 20,000 programmers to work innovating for us.

Top Management's Role

Strategy making is, in some sense, a top-down process. But technology strategy has no meaning until it is embedded in the minds and the hearts of those who must execute it. Corporate edicts have grave limitations. If these people don't believe the strategy or if they don't understand it, it isn't going to be executed. Nothing will happen except that the CEO's credibility will suffer. Yet, like everybody else, I want to exhort the CEO to be the role model for innovation. And we can all think of examples in which the CEO did so.

One of the most important contributions a CEO can make to innovation is management of timing. Thus, while IBM made the decision to go into the personal computer business just twelve months before production started, our top management had been exploring and testing and preparing for our entry into what eventually became consumer electronics for the previous six or seven years. Along the way, we got into and out of the video disc business. We had a variety of in-house projects of a technical variety, of a planning variety, of a market-study variety, in the personal computer business. It was not until we thought we had a reasonable understanding of what the business was, and how it could be institutionalized internally so that it would be free of the old ways of doing things that the project was launched.

Action, Integration

Technology strategy must be embodied in action, not in documents. It has to be there in the venture units, in the joint ventures and the advanced technology projects, in the university collaborations, in the research. Execution is more important than planning.

It is always tempting to try to isolate technology factors from other business issues. Go to a technology executive responsible for these factors and measure that individual as everybody else is measured. That is too neat. It doesn't work well, because technology judgment is involved in almost every business decision we make. Hence the need to involve the technical perspective in a broad range of corporate strategic thinking. By the way, although almost all of IBM's senior executives come from a financial and marketing background, all of them had development and manufacturing management responsibilities before they reached the corporate office.

Planning should not be a staff function, but plans should be subjected to staff debate and review. The line organization must do the planning because that line organization contains the technical community that must own the plan. That applies, of course, to the senior management as well.

Know Your Business Well

My parting message takes the form of an anecdote. A large company—not IBM—had a very successful experience in divesting some businesses that were worth more to others than to them. At a board meeting, one of the outside directors suggested that the role of top management is to be a portfolio manager. It was suggested that the CEO should identify businesses in the company that are meeting corporate objectives but from a strategic point of view might be worth more to somebody else than they are to that company. These businesses should be put up on the block and, when sold, may generate a lot of cash. And it was even suggested by one director that the steel industry had suffered because managements had mistakenly thought they were supposed to be running steel businesses rather than managing portfolios.

I disagreed. In my opinion, the primary role of the chief executive is to know more about his company's industry than any other human being on the face of the earth. Next, the CEO has to motivate the people in his company to know more about their pieces of that business than anybody else. Managing portfolios ranks third. Everybody looked at me as if I were the kid who spoiled the party. We went to another subject. At the end of the meeting, the senior vice president for development came up and hugged me.

Chapter 23
Questions and Answers

Question for Mr. Cooper: Is your long-range planning by product line or by technical function?

MR. COOPER: Some of both. We have created what we call a long-range technology planning system which is technology oriented. We want to understand everything about that technology regardless of what the product application is, and use whatever experts we have throughout the company. Incidentally, what happens is that these experts end up teaching each other. On the other hand, that technology plan is accessible to the people who are creating their business-technology plans. And they incorporate this into their technology road-maps.

Question for Dr. Branscomb: What are the key factors in successful transfer of technology from corporate research to operating divisions?

DR. BRANSCOMB: People. The most successful technology transfer is to move the team that did the advance research into development to carry it out, to move the development team into manufacturing to build it. But that is a lot easier said than done. Technical people only perform well when they are in their usual environments. Development people do not develop well in research; research people don't research well in development.

Alternatives have to be found, therefore. One alternative that we use is the sabbatical. Our research directors work very hard to encourage their senior technical people, especially the ones who set the role models in research, to take a sabbatical in one of the development laboratories. This shows the rest of the research organization that pride or reputation will not be lost by working with the engineers instead of taking a sabbatical at a university.

Second, we make extensive use of task forces or special study groups—full-time efforts for 30 or 60 days—with joint teams from the two sides. Almost all new questions are addressed by task forces.

Third, we find it essential to conduct some applied and problem-focused activities in corporate research, and perhaps more important, to carry out exploratory technology activities and some exploratory product idea activities in the development organization. This produces an umbilical cord in both organizations working at the same level of economic test or speculation. There has to be a piece of the same culture in both organizations to knit them together.

MR. COOPER: Everything that Lew Branscomb says is also true in our organization. And we have had some success in persuading our central research people that they are not successful until whatever it is that they're working on has been moved from under their aegis. For them to create a product has absolutely no significance if somebody doesn't steal it from them. Through our use of motivational tools like bonuses and salaries to convince them that this is their role in life, they have become pretty good marketers. They go out and sell the results of their research to development and to the product groups.

DR. BRANSCOMB: One more thought: The question of how much money is spent in corporate research is, as I said before, a subjective judgment by top management. We look at what they had last year and give them a cost-of-operations adjustment; and then we give them a delta up or a delta down, depending on whether or not they've done a good job with application transfer activities. And if we have advanced technology programs in the development laboratories which are also exploratory in character, we will judge resource levels in part according to how well they have done in reaching out to research and other sources of new ideas. This is a powerful incentive.

CHAIRMAN GAVIN: Our practices are similar. We move people around; we form task forces. Some of our research people have proved to be extremely good program engineers. And moving them around gives them a broader view. One thing to watch out for is that not everybody can do everything. But within that bound, it does work.

Question for Dr. Branscomb: IBM is funding several National Science Foundation university-industry research centers. Which of the seven generations of IBM products have been studied at these cooperative research centers?

DR. BRANSCOMB: There is a welding technology center at Ohio State University, and others that NSF has been involved in through its university-industry program, and we participate. Most of those are aimed at base technologies that will be useful in manufacturing development and sometimes even in research. But none of those investments are aimed at benefiting any particular cycle in our activity or any particular development.

Much more significant are university projects that we fund without the involvement of the government, like a major project we have at Carnegie-Mellon University and another major one at MIT, both at the multimillion-dollar level. These are clearly aimed at what I call product levels five or six. Remember, the generations are but two or three years apart.

Question for Mr. Cooper and Dr. Branscomb: Just how do you avoid the NIH (not-invented-here) factor?

MR. COOPER: You don't avoid it. NIH exists, and to a certain extent it is desirable, because the NIH people are sometimes the innovators, the people with strength. All one can do is reward the people who do innovate. And use a lot of persuasion, intimidation, seminars and technology meetings to encourage transfer of technology in the company.

DR. BRANSCOMB: One of our strategies is to try to maintain a very low profile on the part of the Corporate Technical Committee. Since we spend years trying to cajole people into changing their attitudes, it is desperately important, when they finally do so, that they believe they have done this on their own. And we actively try to inculcate that in the way we do our work. That is one reason why most members of the Corporate Technical Committee only serve one year. It is a no-glory operation.

Question for Mr. Cooper and Dr. Branscomb: Is buying a company a good way to improve or expand R&D or technology capability?

MR. COOPER: In buying a company, one acquires specific resources. If some of those resources are capable R&D or technical people or a patent portfolio or a product line, the significant issue is one of value. Buying a company is a very costly but very quick way of acquiring technology. The same thing can be accomplished at much lower cost—but over a much longer time—by acquiring people and executing the technology in-house. The answer comes down to a time versus money issue, and is obviously different for every specific case.

DR. BRANSCOMB: From IBM's perspective, I have to answer that question this way: I wish I knew. Buying companies is not something we are encouraged to do by the government. From what I know about two other companies, I think that buying a company to get a technology does not make a lot of sense. Technology is too perishable. But buying a company to learn a new business may be very important, if management has the good judgment to let the people who are running it continue to run it until management has really learned what it is they know.

Question for Mr. Cooper and Dr. Branscomb: How do your companies take into account the tendency for scientists and engineers to lose their expertise? Does this happen to lawyers or accountants?

MR. COOPER: I don't believe that people lose their expertise. Yes, they do get stale, and it is incumbent upon the management to create an environment in which people are encouraged to keep learning and to keep doing different kinds of things. But the fact is that the human mind retains its ability to learn and retains its ability to create so long as it is exercised. So I would suggest that if people have become obsolete, it is very likely because they have not been permitted to continue learning, to continue exercising their minds. To put it more bluntly, they've been boxed into situations where they don't have the opportunity to do these things.

We generally do not have this problem, although it does manifest itself among individuals occasionally. When it does, it is not because technologies have changed, but because the people have elected not to keep learning, to keep their minds trained.

DR. BRANSCOMB: I think the difference between the engineers and the accountants is that it is much harder to keep up with the IEEE than it is with the FASB. There is a lot more going on in engineering than in accounting. But the real nub of the issue is exactly as Mr. Cooper puts it: It is career management of the individual. I think first-level managers have the biggest responsibility and are the biggest source of difficulty. The problem is not the deadwood engineer, the poor fellow who struggles to keep up. Rather the issue is the destruction of the best people in the house. This happens if a first-level manager finds out such a person is a whizbang at something, and the manager keeps that individual doing that something over and over and over again. After the third time, the person is bored and is four years behind weaker rivals in the company who have had the career-developing experience of being assigned to new projects. So the issue comes right down to people management.

A subsidiary comment: This is a worse problem for engineers than it is for scientists. The reason is that scientists in the research laboratory have persuaded their management that they must be allowed to win the personal gratification that flows from the respect of their peers. So research managers are obliged to encourage these scientists to belong to professional societies, to give papers and have them published, to be reviewed by peers, to win professional awards. Unfortunately engineers, by and large, don't get such opportunities to the same extent. But they live on ego, too—a point made very nicely by John Bridges. Feeding these egos pays off. Tell them they have to belong to the professional society and go to meetings. Don't tell them they can't because they can't be spared for an afternoon.

CHAIRMAN GAVIN: I'll certainly agree with that. In fact, all too often engineers are told to spend 30 seconds thinking about our recent success before we move onto the next crisis. I've done that myself and it is good for a quick laugh but, all too often, that is the fate of the engineer. There is a continuing requirement for renewal among engineers, whether it is formal or informal. I was in the last class at MIT that worried about biplanes. Times do change.

* * *

I would like to highlight some things that have not been said. One is the matter of project selection. It is impossible to do all those interesting things that one would like to do, so a weeding out process is essential. And this can take place all the way from the grass-roots level right up to the boardroom; it should not be limited to any one segment of a company.

The second thing that nobody has highlighted is the need for management to distinguish between experts and innovators. They are not the same kind of people. If you are lucky, you have both. The number of innovators generally is not as large as those who would claim to be experts.

Next, any organization develops inertia. It tends to become accustomed to what it is doing. Committees are formed, and inertia sets in. It is necessary to move people, change internal structures to avoid the inhibiting, even choking, growth of inertia.

Another subject worth attention is often overlooked: corporate personality. I come from an organization where the principal interest over the years has been defying gravity. And when one defies gravity on a daily basis, one becomes extraordinarily conservative in some respects and extraordinarily radical in other respects. Our particular combination of conservatism and radicalism is probably quite different from what one would find at IBM or Motorola. Although I've only mentioned one influence on corporate personality, there are many others. Don't lose sight of them—or it.

Part VIII
Looking Ahead

Chairman: Joseph G. Gavin, Jr.
President and Chief Operating Officer
Grumman Corporation

Chapter 24
Science, Technology and Education in the Future

David S. Saxon
President
University of California

In an article titled "Economic Futures," the author described several recent attempts to predict the direction our economy will take in the months and years ahead. He referred to ancient times, when it began: "... the world was rife with men who heard voices in the air, saw faces in the skies, and knew what the future held. Today we have many, much more down to earth, of course, who perceive the future in their charts [and] tables.... They are often, though not always, professors.[1]

If it is true that academics have a greater tendency than the rest of the population to believe in the soundness of their own projections, it is a tendency that I intend to resist in my assessment of what lies ahead for science and technology. Indeed, I must begin on a cautionary note: If experience has taught us anything, it is that attempts to predict the future—even the relatively short-term future—turn out to be largely failures, and the more detailed the prediction, the more complete the failure.

Yet we are certainly better off thinking about our future than ignoring it, provided we do not take our predictions too literally and that we focus on broad, rather than on specific, themes. Given those caveats, what can we reasonably say about the future of U.S. science and technology over the next years and decades?

My response to that question is to identify a number of developments that I think are both likely and important, some of which even seem likely to be ripe for exploitation and application. However, there is one overriding development that I regard as not merely likely but cer-

tain: Our society and our world, already technological in character, are on a one-way track; they will become more and more technological, irreversibly.

The End of an Era

Before talking about what the future holds for science and technology, we need to understand the environment and circumstances out of which that future will evolve. An amazingly productive era is now coming to an end, an era that can be traced to the Second World War in two senses. Political repression in Europe before and during the war led to a large influx of brilliantly talented scientists into the United States—Einstein and Fermi, von Neumann and Bethe, to name just a few—whose pioneering scientific work helped to establish the United States as an international center of research and development. In addition, the contributions of new kinds of scientific knowledge—in nuclear physics and in solid-state physics, for example—and the new skills developed by physicists working in these fields turned out to have direct, immediate, and often unanticipated—but critically important—applications to the war effort. The Manhattan Project is the most famous example, but there are others. Because basic science and the applications it made possible turned out to be absolutely vital to our survival, many people became convinced that it was essential to the national interest that a framework for systematically encouraging support of science be established when the war had ended.

The man who sketched out that framework was Vannevar Bush, whose report *Science, The Endless Frontier* proposed that the Federal Government un-

[1]Melville J. Ulmer, "Economic Futures." *Commentary,* February, 1983, p. 50.

derwrite basic research on a scale undreamed of before.[2] Bush's work was the first step toward the establishment of a new and spectacularly productive alliance between universities and government. As Bush predicted, the benefits have been not only scientific and educational but economic as well. Much of the so-called high-technology sector has been brought into being, and almost all of industry has been revolutionized, by science-based developments since world War II—computers, electronics, lasers, pharmaceuticals, and more.

But the wave generated by the war has now largely spent itself. Most of the great European scientists of the war era have died or retired. The enthusiastic commitment of the Federal Government to support basic research in universities has ebbed for a variety of reasons, some having to do with the economic troubles of recent times and some with other kinds of strains that have developed in the relationship between universities and the Federal Government during the past decade or so. Further, we have lost confidence in our ability to be productive and innovative, in our ability to compete successfully with Japan or with Germany. Accordingly, there are many who view the future of science and technology in this country with despair. I am not among their number. I am among those who believe that we stand on the verge of remarkable and perhaps unparalleled developments and opportunities—mainly scientific and technological in character—that we stand, as the phrase goes, at a hinge of history.

Reasons for Optimism about the Future

I have a number of reasons for my optimism about the future. The first is our natural resources, the fact that we are among the most richly endowed countries in the world. What the Japanese have shown is that human intelligence, even without the assistance of abundant natural resources, can create a productive and competitive economy. How much greater is our own potential, given the natural wealth we have to work with?

My second reason for optimism about the future is the fundamental strength and quality of the basic research performed in this country. The fact that U.S. science is decentralized—performed not just in national institutes but in industry and in universities as well—has endowed the scientific enterprise in this country with unparalleled vigor and resiliency. When I talk to Japanese visitors, for example, I am often struck by just how keenly they feel the difference between their capabilities for performing basic research and ours, and by how economically

vulnerable they consider themselves to be as a result of their creative weakness in this area.

Third, we have a great advantage over most other nations in our traditional willingness to experiment, to innovate, to take and accept risks in devising new arrangements, such as the many experiments already going on between universities and industry in support of research. This is entirely unsurprising, given the American tendency to welcome new ideas and new techiques. The ingrained optimism of Americans, so often a puzzle to foreign visitors, will surely serve us well if it continues to encourage innovative arrangements for performing research, both basic and applied.

Fourth, we have an equally important source of strength in the diversity of our institutions—educational, industrial, governmental. This diversity has meant that we are not committed to any one way of accomplishing our aims, whether they be educating our young people, running our industries, or governing ourselves. On the contrary, we have many sources of new ideas and new approaches to our national problems, including the problem of seeing that we invest in the future through research and development.

Finally, I think the future is bright because the most exciting developments in both applied science and technology have been and still are overwhelmingly American. We are the major source of new developments and new discoveries, of new understandings of nature and of new applications of such understandings. In that regard we are still the envy of the world.

What does the future look like from the perspective of these uniquely American strengths?

What Lies Ahead

First of all, it seems clear to me that the search for new and deeper understandings of nature will continue to engage us, even though practical applications may often be remote and even unlikely.

In Physics...

Let me start with my own discipline, physics, the scope of which I interpret broadly. Probably the deepest and most challenging, and in many ways the most exciting, work is on what I call the external frontier of physics: the edge of what is known, where we try to extrapolate from what we know, about the universe, to what we don't know, to go from the laws of nature we understand, to those as yet undiscovered.

I am referring dominantly to work on elementary particles, on the character of the fundamental forces that govern their interactions, and on unified theories that try to link these fundamental forces. This sort of inquiry has been pursued for more than 2,000 years. One can trace interest in these questions from the Greek philosophers, who tried to comprehend the world in a unified way, through Bacon, Newton, and, of course, Einstein.

[2]Vannevar Bush, *Science, The Endless Frontier, a Report to the President on a Program for Postwar Scientific Research*. Washington, D.C.: U.S. Office of Scientific Research and Development, U.S. Government Printing Office, 1945; reprinted by the National Science Foundation, 1980.

At the present time, we are making great progress. There have been grand unifications in the past—for instance, of electricity and magnetism by Maxwell, which then immediately led to the further incorporation of all optics and light into that single unified theory. The most spectacular recent result has been the unification of these electromagnetic interactions and the weak interactions of nuclear physics in a single theory. This theory predicted that there ought to be some specific new particles and these new particles have recently been discovered. It is indeed spectacular when a previously unimagined phenomenon is predicted, then turns out to actually exist.

Present efforts focus on extending that framework to embrace the strong interactions, the interactions that deal with the elementary particles at the nuclear and sub-nuclear level. There is a serious difficulty associated with these efforts because they take us outside the domain of what is experimentally observable. And, the minute physics cannot experiment, it stops being physics.

There are two ways by which we may be able to surmount this dilemma. First, in these grand unified theories that bring together three of the four known forces, one of the predictions is that ordinary matter, of which you and I and everything else is made, is unstable, even though there is no obvious indication that it is. (As a matter of fact, every indication is just the opposite.) This predicted instability of matter takes place on a time scale of 10^{31} years at least, much greater than the mere 30-billion-year age of the universe. Right now there are experiments under way—some of them in deep salt mines—to ascertain whether or not ordinary matter does decay. What has to be done is to assemble a tremendous amount of massive material and screen out all extraneous events (very difficult); then try to observe the extremely rare decay events that the theories postulate.

The second potentially promising way around the dilemma of experimental nonobservability of the consequences of grand unified theories lies in the field of cosmology, to which I will return later.

Here is where we stand with respect to these theories. We have had some great recent successes but we are in a highly speculative phase now, quite disconnected with experiment. We may not see any new breakthroughs for decades or more, depending on these stability experiments. In any event, what I said earlier bears repeating: None of this work is likely to lead to practical applications, yet it responds to a tenacious and deep-seated human need to know and understand the world.

What I call the internal frontier of physics is a complementary area, and one certain to lead to many important practical results. Here we apply the known laws of nature to new situations and circumstances, but circumstances so complex and so far removed from past experience that we are often unable to predict the outcome in advance. For example, we may know the laws that govern the behavior and the properties of isolated atoms and molecules and particles, but that does not mean we can predict the properties of large aggregates and mixtures of such entities in close association, as in ordinary matter or in plasmas. This particular domain is usually called "condensed matter physics." One can imagine—perhaps even foresee—remarkable developments. Can we construct materials that melt at far higher temperatures than anything now known, or that are superconductors of electricity at far higher temperatures than are the known superconductors, materials that are harder or tougher? What new kinds of surfaces can we construct (catalysis) and what new kinds of molecules (chemistry)? How far, to put it more generally, can we go, within the laws of physics, before we reach the limits of what a material can be made to be or do? This is a continuously evolving field in which important advances will occur with certainty.

Not all will happen soon, however. *Fusion* is an example of major importance. We already know all the laws of physics we need to know in order to make a thermonuclear fusion reaction occur. But the real problem is how to make it occur on a large scale in a controlled way, how to go from the microscopic to the macroscopic domain. And, of course, when the terribly difficult technical problems are solved—and I have no doubt they eventually will be, in 25 or 50 years perhaps—the political and social problems associated with nuclear energy of all kinds will likely remain. I will not even hazard a guess about the time scale required for those problems to work themselves out.

I want to mention two other domains of physics. One is the linking of astrophysics, cosmology and general relativity. General relativity is a subject that has been with us since 1915, but only recently has it become an integral part of physics because only recently have we been able to make pertinent observations. Astrophysical and cosmological phenomena and general relativity are coming together now as a result of recent technological advances. One, of course, is the computer, which permits us to correlate observations, to get coherent data from antennae separated from one another by huge distances. A second is the space observatory that is soon to be put in orbit. This will make the universe far more accessible to observation than in the past.

The last domain of physics I shall mention is the study of the origin of the universe. The "big bang" in some ways is the ultimate laboratory, for every aspect of physics is present in the process of the big bang: elementary particle physics, the interrelations among the forces, condensed matter. The evolution of the universe from that starting point provides us with evidence, admittedly tenuous and remote, of what was happening at the beginning. And that is the sense in which, as we continue more fully to understand cosmology, we may begin to learn new things about the elementary particles. That is the one hope, besides the work involving the decay of matter, that I see in testing grand unified theories. It is an interesting connection: the absolutely most microscopic and most macroscopic being joined together at the moment of the big bang.

I must add that stars themselves are an extreme form of condensed matter from which we can learn much. Neutron stars are spectacular examples. And, of course, the sun is a fusion device.

In Mathematics...

There has been a big advance in nonlinear mathematics in the last few years, an advance which has major implications. Almost all the developments in mathematics over the centuries have been in linear mathematics, which, at best, is an approximation of the real world because the real world is nonlinear. We have never been able to deal with nonlinear problems in a systematic way. That has now changed. I think we are going to see many developments in nonlinear mathematics, which a few years ago would have been thought absolutely beyond the capacity of anyone to deal with. These developments will permit us to see the real world in a completely new way. We are already, for instance, beginning to understand the puzzle of deterministic systems exhibiting chaotic behavior. Fluid mechanics offers arresting examples of this puzzle: how ocean waves break; how drops from a dripping faucet are distributed when they strike a surface.

I think that the importance of this is twofold. First, the problems that are being worked on are already interesting from a practical point of view. Second, like all major advances, it changes the attitudes of people who work in the field. One might ask, has the four-minute mile of mathematics now been run? My answer is yes—a cautiously confident yes.

I have discussed two sets of future potentialities. One concerns speculations about the fundamental nature of the universe and, while this work is unlikely to generate any practical applications, it nonetheless adds an important dimension to our understanding of experience. The second set revolves around such areas as condensed matter physics and nonlinear mathematics which, although they are certain to have important applications, are not likely to produce major surprises. But what about those fields where spectacular breakthroughs have already occurred and where other breakthroughs seem to be at hand? What are their possibilities and limits, and what do they suggest about the future character of our society?

In Information Technology...

Progress in analyzing, storing and calling up vast amounts of information has recently been so rapid and so startling that it has dominated the public's imagination. One dimension of this accelerating process has been our increasing ability to store and process more and more

information on smaller and smaller chips at lower and lower costs. Speculation about the future of information technology has tended to revolve around the question of how much further we can go in improving the processing power of a microchip. Faster, smaller, cheaper, more powerful; minis and supers. What are the limits? One is set by the speed of light, which puts an absolute limit on how fast a computer can process information. Another is the minimum size that can be attained for a single element and the maximum possible density achievable for these elements. Here the human brain is a guide to the limit: 10^{12} or so elements (neurons) in an object the size of our heads.

These are technical limits, however, and they do not reflect a different and most fascinating aspect of our enormously increased capacity to handle information. More interesting than the purely technical problems is the broader question of what we do with the information we have now learned to store and process. Many people assume that information is an absolute good, that the more we have, the better off we are. That is not true. Unsorted and unanalyzed information can be anywhere from useless to harmful, which is why we automatically screen out much of the sensory data that come to us from our environment.

An important next step in information technology, therefore, is building a computer that knows how to use the information it stores. In fact, that step is already under way. Early this Spring, the Japanese announced their intention of building an "intelligent" computer by 1990, one that will be able to converse with people in nontechnical language, summarize conversations for future use, and highlight important points in reading materials. Here in the United States, several companies are said to be experimenting with what is called "expert systems"—computers that, like human experts, combined textbook knowledge with experience, and then make informed guesses about situations.

Whether or not the Japanese reach their goal by 1990, the development of artificial intelligence is a driving goal in the field of information technology—a possibility that has inspired such different visions of the future as the film *2001* and the world of Asimov's benign robots. And the most exciting aspect of this development, it seems to me, is once again not the strictly technical challenge but the possibility it offers for learning about human intelligence and how the brain works. John von Neumann—the man who did so much to make the computer age possible—thought from the very beginning that such reciprocal kinds of learning were possible, that an understanding of how a computer functions would soon yield greater understanding of how our own brains function. In 1948, he presented his "General and Logical Theory of Automata," in which he laid the foundation that he believed would not only allow us to build better and more sophisticated machines, but would also permit a better understanding of the design and function of living organisms.

That was 35 years ago. We have since learned that it is indeed useful and suggestive to think about some aspects of living organisms in mechanical terms, and vice versa. Thus my suggestion that the brain and its neurons are a guide to the faster, smaller cheaper limits of microchip processing power. In a sense, then, von Neumann's predictions have come true. But the larger truth is that real progress in extrapolating from the functioning of machines to the functioning of human beings lies ahead of us. And that should tell us something about the time scale along which we are able to project; the further away we get from narrowly technical concerns, the more uncertain our ability to predict future developments.

It is, perhaps, appropriate to take note of a striking dissimilarity between the human brain and the modern computer, a dissimilarity in the path of evolution and the path we have taken in developing computers. With the latter, we have emphasized high-speed, sequential operations. The brain does not operate in billionths of a second—or in millionths. It operates much more slowly, and it processes information in a completely different way from computers. Apparently the brain works through multiple connections, by parallel processing, as contrasted with the linear method by which we make computers work.

...And in Biotechnology

In discussing biotechnology, I move farther and farther away from topics about which I know something. It has been wisely remarked that it is imprudent to speak on subjects about which one knows nothing. But how can one speak about the future at all if one takes that dictum too seriously or literally?

To put the development of biotechnology into some perspective, it is important, first of all, to realize that we have already been at work in the field for some 30 years. I realize most people have the feeling that biotechnology is something that happened two years ago or maybe even three years ago. That is not true. The double helix was discovered in 1953. The genetic code was "cracked" in 1966. Gene splicing was discovered in 1972, almost 20 years after the double-helix milestone. One of the discoverers of the double helix, James Watson, has said no one could have predicted gene splicing even a year before it was demonstrated. It came as a total surprise to those who had been working in the field for two decades.

This story tells us something about both breakthroughs and their predictability. Perhaps one can predict orderly evolutionary outcomes, but not breakthroughs.

What is new and immediate in biotechnology is the scope and intensity of the effort, across a broad front, to exploit the potentialities of the field as we now perceive them—for human health and welfare, for new and

startling technologies, for understanding nature and the nature of life. I am going to focus my remarks on some of these potentialities for agriculture. I am mindful, of course, of the significance of work in other domains—work on genetics and genetic structure, on the identification of specific genetic sites for specific characteristics of plant or animal, on cancer mechanisms and cancer-causing genes, on the production of useful substances by tailor-made bacteria, and much more. But I choose agriculture partly because it tends not to be viewed as biotechnologically exciting and partly because agriculture is largely free of the moral, ethical and social dilemmas associated with biotechnological developments affecting human beings or animals. Therefore, it is likely, I believe, to see the earliest application of advances presently unimaginable; such advances, however, still being decades away in my view.

The essential points are simply stated when it comes to the agricultural applications of biotechnology. The first is our newfound ability to introduce entirely different genetic materials into plants. The second is our ability to identify quickly and accurately the characteristics of the new plants that result. And the third is our ability to rapidly reproduce genetically identical plants.

The essential consequence is equally simple to state. We are going to be able to speed up enormously our ability to select for a presently inconceivably broad range of plant characteristics. We have already started. For example, work is underway on the development of salt-tolerant plants, plants that can grow in brackish or salty water, as well as for the development of disease and pest-resistant plants, and of plants that can fix nitrogen. The eventual impact of such developments on agricultural productivity and on the use of our natural resources is beyond measure, but it is only the beginning.

After all, we are already familiar with plants that fix nitrogen and others that are salt-tolerant. We know that some plants are naturally disease-resistant and others sufficiently pest-resistant that we grind them into insecticide powders. So the examples I have mentioned, exciting as they are, would merely extend what already exists in nature, what nature itself tells us is possible. Who knows what other characteristics, entirely new, different and unknown, will emerge from the further application of these developments? Who among us can conceive of them?

And what of the other areas of application of biotechnology? I have no doubt that we will ultimately be able to deal completely with cancer, as we also will with impairments resulting from genetic deficiencies. But how will we make use of the clue that nature gives us when it provides examples of animals which can produce new tails or new limbs or even new halves of themselves? Animals with cells which know when to reproduce so as to generate new parts and, just as important, when to stop. What new and entirely different kinds of creatures will be possible? And who will have the wisdom to choose?

Interactions and Other Matters

To complete this brief, highly personal tour of future developments in four fields of science and technology, I would stress that interactions among these fields will prove to be increasingly significant. There will be a linking of physics, mathematics, information technology, and biotechnology in as yet unimagined—even unimaginable—ways. In the realm of the imaginable, we may envision the use of biotechnology to create integrated circuits at the molecular biological level, or to create "organic factories" without the intervention or presence of mechanical processes. We already have prototypes of organic factories: trees, cows and the development of bacteria to produce interferon.

I am constrained to mention, but not make any predictions about, the possibility of extraterrestrial intelligence. This *Buck Rogers* or *Star Wars* field of inquiry has occupied, and doubtless will continue to occupy, some of our very best minds.

A recurring theme of these remarks has been limits— the limits of scientific and technological developments imposed by the laws of nature—those we know, those we have yet to discover.[3] But, of course, there are other limits that will constrain our application of these developments: social, political, ethical and environmental limits. They surely will command our attention.

The Educational Challenge

All these developments will produce transformations on an inconceivable scale, qualitatively and quantitatively, surely not less than those produced by the invention of the printing press and by the industrial revolution. Among other things, this means that our world, already technological (and nuclear), will become more and more technological as the future unfolds. There is no going back.

The developments I have described will certainly be reflected in our schools and universities, in the classroom and in the laboratory. Computers, video displays, disks, cassettes, lasers, optical fibers, satellites and the like will give unprecedented access to bibliographical and other kinds of information. Such predictions already have an old-fashioned ring, because they have been made over and over again since television and computers were first introduced. In fact, of course, such devices have not taken over the classroom or laboratory and probably never will, but they will surely become an increasingly common and routine element in the way teaching and learning take place.

However, my intent is not to make predictions about educational technology but to assert what education itself must become if, in fact, we are going to be able, as a society, to accommodate to the transformations I have been describing.

Despite our national preoccupation with technology (infatuation with gadgets might be more accurate), we are and have been doing an absolutely terrible job of educating our citizens about matters scientific and technological—in our schools and, except for professionals, in our colleges and universities as well. People embrace new inventions and new devices even as they worry that technology will shorten their lives and ruin their planet. People—including those most educated of Americans, our college graduates—are quite unable to exercise informed judgments when it comes to almost any question connected with science and technology. People are at the mercy of experts or, worse, of charlatans posing as experts. People are unable to exercise their full responsibilities as educated citizens in a society that is not only democratic, but is technological as well. And, unless we do something about our scientific illiteracy, unless we see to it that our citizens come to understand both the power and the limits of science and technology, things will only get worse as the technological character of our society becomes more deeply ingrained.

But that is only half the story. It is at least as urgent, and in some ways even more urgent, that we give our scientists and engineers what they too seldom get from their education now: a sense of the richness and importance of kinds of learning other than scientific and technical knowledge. An education that incorporates a genuinely broad perspective on the world is not important just to individual students. Whether we like it or not, we will become increasingly dependent on those with scientific and technological expertise in the years ahead. I am made uneasy at the prospect of a future that depends on experts too narrowly trained, on mere technicians, on people who are less broadly educated than they are capable of being, on those who cannot and do not understand that knowledge must be tempered by wisdom.

I am not under the illusion that these educational transformations will be easy or quick, or even that we know just how to bring them about. Providing a genuinely liberal education for our students in these times—which is what I am advocating—will obviously be a demanding, long-term task. But we must not be deterred. Our capacity as individuals and as a society to be as ready as we must for a future of unknown and unknowable eventualities demands that kind of education. And we had better get on with the job.

---

[3]Richard Foster covered some specific limits in the development and application of technology, see pages 72-75.

In any event, we can be sure that the future will demand an extraordinary degree of flexibility from all of us, an ability to keep our balance and even to flourish in a world in which change is pervasive and profound. So it is all the more important for us to give our young people the kind of education that will permit them to respond, rather than to submit, to change. Our greater understanding of the physical world holds out enormous potential for improving human life. But the technology that understanding has created will fall with a heavy hand on those who have never learned to comprehend or use it. Only education can show them how.

Chapter 25
Concluding Remarks by Conference Chairman Robert A. Charpie

What have we learned and what conclusions should we draw from this meeting? In responding to these questions, I propose to address myself to the chief executive officers and senior managers in the audience rather than the R&D community. I submit the following:

First, we all should be prepared to agree that our technical assets are our most precious corporate assets. They underlie product leadership, low costs, and the prospects for growth, which, after all, are the textbook ingredients for business success.

Second, new technology will continue to grow relentlessly; that point has been made over and over again. Probably technology will continue doubling in scope every seven to ten years, at least for the rest of this century. Whether we like it or not, that is going to happen, in good times and bad alike. At the national level, technology's success will continue to be a proxy for leadership in the community of nations. And access to this bourgeoning technology will be ever extended until it becomes worldwide.

Third, in a decade of sharply reduced economic growth, the relentless growth of technology and the concomitant demands that will be made on our companies will be hard to accommodate, difficult to finance, troublesome to manage. We shall be tempted to slow down the stroke, to stretch out the risky programs. But the most threatening competition is directed at the heart of our advanced technology. For these competitors, "today the United States, tomorrow the world" is a sure-fire formula for securing domination around the world.

Fourth, the requirement for managing technology better is magnified. Our national well-being will, in fact, be determined by our performance in those technological developments that underpin our military security, our economic security, and economic growth.

Five, what are our responsibilities? The chorus of counsel offered in this conference is clear and constant. It is that a conviction to pay attention to basics is required. To me, this means focusing highest corporate priority on the simple reality that the best technology, when combined with superior management, produces the best products and the lowest cost—a sure recipe for success.

This conference has been addressed to operating management. The message is: Invigorate our competitive spirit by leading technology development; drive forward aggressively to innovate new business opportunities rooted in that new technology; identify, support and, I would add, make rich, successful risk takers, entrepreneurs and innovators; maintain or regain our leadership edge in innovation and the technical fields that sustain our military and our economic security.

In an era of low economic growth around the world, it will take tough-minded visionary managements to hold steady to the course I have prescribed. The remedy proposed is for neither the faint-hearted nor the short-winded. But the prospect of a world in the 21st century suddenly denied U.S. leadership is very threatening and troubling to me.

In reality, we have only a single asset to use in shouldering our responsibilities. That asset is the thousands of successful U.S. business enterprises whose taproots of strength are a blend of appropriate ethical values, competitive energy, and, indispensibly, superior technology.

Chief executives must be prepared to stay the new technology course, even in hard times. We must nurture new technology and identify the people best-equipped to exploit it successfully.

My urgent suggestion is: Let us all go back to work and get with it.